W9-BNS-003

Wedding Planning for the Busy Feminist

AMANDA PENDOLINO

Copyright © 2018 Amanda Pendolino

Cover design by Megan Greydanus
greydanusdesign.com

All rights reserved.

ISBN:
9781980821885

CONTENTS

ACKNOWLEDGMENTS

Thank you to all the wonderful brides and grooms – personal friends and internet strangers – who spoke to me about their wedding disasters and triumphs.

I also could not have written this book without Katie and Maria, the awesome BFF and sister who were smart/crazy enough to name me their Maid of Honor. Thank you for answering all my questions, providing insight on everything and trusting me with a microphone!

I'd also like to thank Lisa Frye, Megan Greydanus, Jeff Willis and Jenna Hidinger.

Finally, thank you to my parents, who encourage me to follow my creative dreams and only pester me about my marital status 1-3 times per year.

INTRODUCTION

Hello!

My name is Amanda, and I'm here to help you plan your wedding. I'm not engaged or married. My dad says this is because I'm "focused on my career," but we'll save that for my next book and/or therapist! I KNOW WHAT YOU'RE THINKING: who is this crazy spinster with the nice hair and why should I listen to her? (Aw, thanks!) Think of me as your second Maid of Honor. A Maid of Honor who has been to every wedding and who has read the entire internet. And who won't push you around with that annoying sentence, "At MY wedding…"

From 2006 to 2016, I attended eight weddings in three different states. Weddings for Northern cousins, Southern cousins, former co-workers, high school friends, college friends and one friend I met on a now-defunct networking email board (New Year's Eve weddings are great! I'm so glad I no longer care about networking! I'm sorry I love parentheses so much!). While some women lament they're "always a bridesmaid, never the bride," I was "always a non-bridal party wedding guest, never joined by a date." When I was once asked to record a video message with marriage advice for a bride and groom, I shrugged and said, "Don't listen to me, I'm single!"

Then my best friend and roommate of ten years got engaged and asked me to be her Maid of Honor.

Suddenly, my love of *Say Yes to the Dress* became relevant to actual life! We drooled over dresses, made Pinterest boards of beachy-but-not-exactly-nautical centerpieces and debated ceremony song choices. I still can't believe she didn't let me walk down the aisle to "Where You Lead," the *Gilmore Girls* theme song by Carole King. I mean come ON, whose wedding is this? Oh, right.

1

Next came THE YEAR OF THE WEDDINGS. Besides my best friend's nuptials, I attended five other weddings in 2017 alone. They included Catholic masses, non-religious garden ceremonies, bands, DJs, Malibu beach photos, fancy tents, improvised vows, homemade centerpieces, fireworks, and even photo ops with zebras and camels. I also attended four bachelorette parties, two of which I planned (and one of those was a surprise for a friend who didn't have a bridal party). Las Vegas' *Magic Mike Live* is a scintillating feminist delight, in case you were wondering.

Then my sister got engaged and asked me to be her Maid of Honor, meaning that I served as MOH for her and for my BFF at the very same time. I began planning a third bachelorette bash. I also got save the dates from two more friends and a cousin. It was time for YEAR OF THE WEDDINGS 2. Redux? Reloaded? The Squeakwel? Seriously, how do I have so many cousins? More importantly, how many weddings am I up to? Eighteen? Forty? Is there a punch card? When do I get a free ham sub? Have I mentioned the first wedding I ever attended, when my aunt chose her OTHER five year-old niece to be the flower girl?[1]

The point is…while you should probably not ask me for marriage advice, I fucking know weddings. I've accidentally become an expert! I'm also responsible for the coupling of 2.5 happily married twosomes. The members of the first couple separately read about a networking event I posted on my blog, attended the event, met each other, started dating and later got hitched. Oh, and they became writing partners and now write for a hit TV show on ABC. You're welcome.

Here's the story behind couple two: my aforementioned best friend met her husband because I was shamelessly hitting on his tall, goofy friend one night at the Roosevelt Hotel in Los Angeles. I found the tall one charming because he saved our other friend from face-planting even when he wasn't trying to mack it on her. Chivalry! And when my BFF later reconnected with her now-husband on a dating app, it was I who insisted she go out with him despite her concern that HE WEARS TOO MANY BASEBALL CAPS. You're welcome.

The third couple I'm only counting as half. Back in college, I made friends with a guy when I visited San Diego. I didn't talk to him for years – but then he met a woman named Amanda one night and texted me the next morning, "So nice to meet you!" I wrote back that he had the wrong Amanda. He mistakenly texted me AGAIN, and I was nice enough to point out AGAIN that he needed to text the other chick. Amanda was the fourth-most popular baby name in 1985, so I understand the mix-up. But twice? Come on. This is why you put people in your phone as "KAYLA SEÑOR FROGS" and "BRIAN WEIRD TEETH". Anyway, he and Other Amanda are now

[1] 27 years later, I am DEFINITELY not still bitter about this.

married with two sons and seem happy in Boston or wherever (Thanks, Facebook). I don't know if I can take full matchmaking credit, but if I hadn't texted him back, he probably would have thought that Other Amanda wasn't interested. She ended up vowing to stay with his confused ass for eternity, so I at least get a half. LIKE I SAID, YOU'RE WELCOME. A hairstylist once told me that in the Jewish faith, matching up three couples sends you straight to heaven. I'm so close.

I'm also super conflicted about weddings and maybe you are, too. If you're reading this book, you value lifelong commitment and intimacy. You believe in building a life with a partner. And you know that these things are more important than one day of flowers and dresses - even if you fucking love flowers and dresses as much as I do. You probably also know that a perfect wedding has nothing to do with the strength of a relationship.

You might also find it exhausting that social media has turned our entire lives into curated, inauthentic performances fueled by heart e mojis and the wedding-industrial complex. Writes Megan Garber in *The Atlantic*: "Nuptials, in the pop-cultured conception, are not merely parties, but gauzy exercises in self-expression. They are intricate productions of the theater of the self, performed as a one-time show."[2]

When everyone around you has put their idealized love on display, it's understandable that you'd want to join in and experience that fantasy for yourself. But while some couples are excited to share their specific brand of love, others feel pressured to perform and agonize over each decision. What IS your specific brand of love, and why do you need one at all?

Weddings are also hella expensive, and every dollar you spend on bedazzled robes could be spent on student loan debt, a house down-payment or one of the other insurmountable expenses of millennial life. You know this. It makes you feel at least a little uncomfortable.

But you kinda want the perfect wedding anyway, right?

I GET IT!

In this book, you will never be judged for caring a lot about small things like table numbers or giving zero fucks about big things like bridesmaids. You will never be pressured to spend more or less than you want or to include or exclude any particular wedding tradition. Whether you've been dreaming about your big day since age five or you've only agreed to have a wedding because your mom is threatening to take you out of her will, I'm here to help you enjoy the process and make it easier to get what you want.

---

[2] Garber, Megan. "How 'I Do' Became Performance Art." The Atlantic. 20 July 2017. https://www.theatlantic.com/entertainment/archive/2017/07/how-the-american-wedding-became-performance-art/533733/

I've also surveyed more than thirty brides and grooms about what worked, what didn't and what they wish they had known during wedding planning. Sucks for them, great for you!

There is no single, correct way to have a wedding. Also, cultural and regional traditions and etiquette vary widely. YOU DO YOU is a wedding planning mantra that will serve you well. Say it with me: YOU DO YOU. Definitely say it out loud if you're reading this on a subway or airplane so that strangers give you the side-eye and ask what book you're reading.

YOU DO YOU!

YOU DO YOU AS YOU SAY "I DO"!

Okay, I'm done. Please keep reading this book.

Chapter One

AMERICAN INSANITY

Have weddings become insane?

Yes and no.

According to The Knot's surveyed brides, the average wedding cost in 2017 was $33,391[3]. CostofWedding.com gives slightly lower figures, saying that the average wedding cost in the United States is $25,764 and that while couples, on average, spend between $19,323 and $32,205, most spend less than $10,000[4]. Location matters: The Knot reports that weddings in Manhattan cost an average of $76,944, while weddings in Utah ring in at $18,516.

Couples today opt for weddings with unique guest experiences, even if that means slashing the guest count. The average number of wedding guests has decreased over the years while the average cost per guest has increased to $268, up from $194 in 2009. So couples are inviting fewer people but spending more per guest, indulging in features like late-night snacks, fortune tellers and party games.

Perhaps weddings have changed because we now get married later in life. According to Overflow, in 1958, the average first-time bride and groom were 20 and 23 (respectively) – but by 2015, they were 27 and 29[5]. A wedding is no longer a party thrown by a bride's parents as a way of saying, "Hey, Judy

---

[3] Seaver, Maggie. "The National Average Cost of a Wedding Is $33,391." The Knot. https://www.theknot.com/content/average-wedding-cost-2017

[4] https://www.costofwedding.com/

[5] Chase. "How is the age at which people get married changing in the U.S." *Overflow.Solutions.* 17 October 2017. http://overflow.solutions/demographic-traits/how-is-the-age-at-which-people-get-married-changing-in-the-u-s/

and her Ovaltine addiction are your problems now!" (I assume the 1950s were just a mess of female possession and Ovaltine.)

Now, brides and grooms are adults who've been out in the world for a decade. Many have been partners for years and already live together. Weddings have become celebrations of already-stable relationships, not events marking the beginning of adulthood or even commitment. Because of this, couples have more say in what their weddings are like – and brides and grooms have had a lot of time to think about what they want. If you've been a wedding guest as many times as I have, you've probably already thought about whether you want your wedding to include a photo booth (yes!), dessert bar (yes!) or lobster (what am I, the carpet king of Wisconsin?)[6].

Reality shows and the internet have also made couples realize that wedding options are endless. A quick internet search finds that couples have gotten married while bungee jumping, swimming underwater in a shark tank and sporting painted faces like characters from *The Nightmare Before Christmas*. Maybe those 1950s folks just didn't know what they were missing.

Plus, it's not our fault that all kinds of wedding cottage industries have popped up in the last few decades, from wine bottles that read "Will You Be My Bridesmaid" to cute ring bearer signs with sayings like "Don't Worry, Ladies, I'm Still Single." I'm not here to tell you that you should or shouldn't buy any of these things; I want to help you feel less overwhelmed by it all. Part of wedding planning stress comes from deciding what you want, what you need, what you deserve and what you feel guilty about. Saying yes to everything will blow your budget, but buying the cheapest everything may make you wonder why you're even bothering to pay for a wedding in the first place.

Your grandma might be right if she claims that you're spending more than she did, but people have always spent a lot on weddings. Writes Jenni Avins in *Quartz*: "While 2013's average wedding price tag of $29,548 is pretty staggering, Depression-era couples in the US – when unemployment hovered between 17% and 20% – were no slouches either when it came to wedding spending. The average 1930s spend of $392.30 ($6,481 in today's dollars, adjusted for inflation) may sound modest, but it was worth one quarter of household income back then. Today's costs are closer to half."[7]

If the critics in your life find modern American wedding culture to be indulgent, feel free to drop the following global knowledge: first, a traditional Indian wedding includes multiple events and lasts an average of three days –

---

[6] My cousin's father-in-law is literally the carpet king of Wisconsin, so I learned at a wedding that lobster is delicious!

[7] Avins, Jenni. "The venerable, 80-year tradition of the insanely expensive American wedding." *Quartz*. 2 July 2014. https://qz.com/228518/the-venerable-80-year-tradition-of-the-insanely-expensive-american-wedding/

sometimes even a week. That farewell brunch doesn't seem so crazy now, does it? Second, Chinese brides generally wear two or three different dresses. They walk down the aisle in a slim, embroidered gown called a traditional qipao or cheongsam, wear a more Western-style dress at the reception, and often change into a THIRD cocktail dress at the end of the night!

Even if we spend a lot of money, at least we truly WANT to get married. Most brides and grooms I spoke with told me that they didn't feel pressure from society or their social circles to tie the knot. In fact, multiple people said that they didn't think about marriage until they "met the right person." If our weddings are the result of carefully considered choices and not obligations, isn't that progress?

If you'd rather get an aggressive teeth cleaning than be the center of attention, a wedding might spike your anxiety – but you can avoid traditions that put you in the spotlight. If you love being the center of attention but feel like it's basic or indulgent, remember that it's your wedding and that you are NOT basic because that's a fake sexist term! Plus, your family and friends WANT to celebrate you and shower you with love. What's wrong with embracing that?

But if the financial, traditional or egoistic aspects of weddings still give you pause, you could strive to make your wedding about more than just a party or a joining of two people. You could choose to use only local vendors, female-led businesses or small businesses, for example. You could decorate with ethically-raised flowers and recycled or eco-friendly décor. You could give out fair-trade favors. You could host your reception at a local cultural center, such as a botanical garden, where your venue fee would go towards a nonprofit organization. Even your catering could make you feel good; Homeboy Industries catering in Los Angeles, for example, provides hope, support and training for formerly gang-involved and previously incarcerated men and women.

That said, let's all consider that your wedding doesn't have to be the ultimate achievement of your life. Your wedding doesn't have to be your masterpiece.

Now, let's talk about how to make your wedding your masterpiece!

Chapter Two

SURVIVING THE WEDDING PLANNING PROCESS

So you're engaged – now what?

You might want to take some time to enjoy the news with just your fiancé, but if you're reading this book, you're probably beyond that. Way to fuck that up. Kidding! It's an exciting time! Congrats!

As soon as you announce your engagement, you may get bombarded with questions: When are you getting married? What's your venue? What kind of dress do you want? How many people are you inviting? Will global warming have advanced to the point of making suit jackets optional?

"A lot goes into planning a wedding. The list is endless," says Francesca from New York, NY. "Relax. Enjoy being engaged. It should be such a happy time, but there's a lot of pressure to pick a date and start wedding planning. Once you start, you can't stop. So give yourselves some time to just enjoy being in your love bubble! Don't try to do it all at once."

People will assume they're invited. People will ask for plus-ones! And worse, people will start giving you all kinds of unsolicited advice. Not me! You bought this book, so I'm solicited, baby. But your fun engagement announcement may quickly devolve into your taking care of other people and their expectations.

"I was surprised how many people in our life (family and friends) – usually the most chill people - needed to feel like special flowers when it came to our wedding," says Jen from Los Angeles, CA.

Another bride agrees: "I wish I really knew how much everyone would make it about themselves."

One bride told me that a relative even sent a GROUP email after the wedding to complain about the seating chart!

Weddings can bring out a lot of repressed emotional baggage and weird judgments! Take a breath and remember what's important in the long run: glittery décor. Just kidding. It's marriage or something. To try and remain a Bridechilla, stand up for yourself when you can and vent to your friend or partner when you can't. Wedding planning should be fun! Keep people in the dark about details if they're only going to stress you out with their opinions. Be flexible about parts of the wedding you don't feel strongly about – but it's your wedding, and you can't please everyone.

"My dad brought his own handle of tequila since the wine and beer we offered weren't good enough," says Erin from Los Angeles, CA.

"My least favorite part of wedding planning was trying to manage expectations about traditions that I absolutely did not give a shit about," says Kait from New York, NY. "I wish I had known the weird shit my family cared about."

"You think you're going to be different," says another Los Angeles bride. "You think you won't care about the details and it won't be this big thing. But it's EVERYONE ELSE who turns it into a big thing."

Wedding planning can get especially complicated when family members are paying for some or all of the wedding. Sit down with your parents or step-parents and ask if they plan to contribute. Don't assume that anyone is or isn't paying. I've even heard some stories of couples getting offers of money that were later rescinded! Also, remember that when other people are paying, they may expect to have a say. Depending on your priorities, you might prefer to plan a cheaper wedding that fits your tastes and doesn't include your stepdad's weird golf buddies.

Find out what elements of the wedding are most important to your parents - but be clear about what you want as well.

"Don't get caught up trying to make everyone happy," says Jessica from Cheektowaga, NY. "It's your day, so you and your partner should do what you want, no matter who is paying for it!"

If you're worried that a relative will get too involved, you might be able to satisfy her by including her in particular activities, such as dress shopping; she could also focus on planning a shower.

On the other hand, you might enjoy delegating planning responsibilities to an overzealous friend or family member. "My amazing Mom and Nana planned everything for us, so we only did the fun stuff," says Erica from Glendale, CA. "We just wanted to have a good time and for our guests to have a good time, so we were more than happy to have my Mom and Nana pick out tablecloth colors."

Don't remain engaged for more than a year unless you need time to save money, you have your heart set on a specific date or you want a particular venue that's booked or limited by seasons. Most newlyweds I spoke to found the wedding planning process stressful and were relieved when it was over –

so why make that stretch on longer than necessary? Some also regretted how much time and money they spent planning a relatively short event.

"I wish I would have known how fast the actual day would go by," says a bride from Amherst, NY. I don't know if I would have put so much effort into seven hours if I had known."

"My wedding advice is to plan your honeymoon," says a bride from Portland, Maine. "Three years later, I still haven't taken one!"

Leah from upstate New York agrees: "Don't get caught up in the hype. Take at least 25% of your budget and spend it on your honeymoon instead. The world won't end, and you'll be happier for it. The day will be special no matter what."

If you don't want to think about your wedding every day for your entire engagement, get a new email account to sign up for store promo codes, wedding website accounts, etc. Don't put the inbox on your phone. This way, David's Bridal can't bombard you about dresses and shoes every day – you'll have to actually decide to log in on your computer. Isn't power great?

A wedding planner can also reduce your stress level during wedding planning – something I'll discuss more in Chapter Five. You'll also have a better time planning if you choose your bridal party carefully (see Chapter Seventeen!).

A bride from Buffalo, NY found that securing vendors early on made her feel calm and productive. "It's never too early to make reservations for rehearsal dinners, farewell breakfasts, hotel blocks, transportation and make up," she says. "If you are organized enough, reach out a year in advance, particularly if you live in a smaller city or area where there are fewer vendors. You'll have more choices if you start early."

However, if you find yourself getting behind with wedding planning, don't freak out - you don't need to have everything in place a year in advance. A Los Angeles bride told me she looked for a videographer just three months before her wedding and still had plenty to choose from.

Be honest with yourself about whether you tend to procrastinate or find it stressful to make quick decisions. "It is helpful to prepare and make decisions ahead of time, so you don't feel like you're rushing to pick something or settling on something," says Alissa from Troy, NY. "I am a procrastinator so I felt like I was making a lot of late-in-the-game decisions." She says the best advice she could give an engaged couple is "TIME MANAGEMENT."

This might sound obvious, but please eat. As someone who's made all kinds of almond flour monstrosities, I totally understand if want to lose weight for your wedding. But if you spend an entire year hungry, you're going to be miserable and make everyone else miserable, too. Just because Amazon has 109 different "sweating for the wedding" results doesn't mean you have to buy into a narrative of "I must diet."

If you want to change your eating or workout habits, think about positive ways to do so – finding a workout you enjoy or incorporating more veggies into your diet, for example. Set reasonable goals; instead of "I will get down to my eighth grade weight," maybe it's "Today I will not throw six cookies in the garbage and then eat them anyway."[8] Also, please remember that your partner is marrying you because s/he already loves you the way you are.

Kristin from Woodland Hills, CA says her wedding planner gave her some great advice about dieting. "The best thing she told me was 'Do not diet for your wedding! You don't want photos that you'll always be trying to live up to.' I had bought into the 'wedding diet' bullshit so hard!!! I stopped worrying and wore Spanx and looked and felt great - and more like myself!"

Your self-care regimen might also require limiting your internet searching, since wedding websites can be inspirational but overwhelming. "I definitely felt pressure (put on by myself after looking at wedding websites and Pinterest) to have small 'perfect touches," says Alissa.

Anastasiya from Los Angeles, CA agrees: "Figuring out minutiae like website design and 'unique' gift books or table numbers was the worst because there is so much pressure to have everything be a unique and clever statement about your relationship personality - and it was exhausting." Even the phrase "relationship personality" is exhausting! As much as I love modern weddings, maybe yours could just be a fun party. It's fine if your table numbers are just literal numbers.

Maybe you'll feel less pressure to make every wedding detail perfect if you allow yourself some indulgences in everyday life. I'm not saying we can all afford eyelash extensions on the reg[9], but maybe if you bought yourself flowers or got a dress tailored once in a while, your wedding wouldn't feel like the ONLY time in your life you get to experience these things.

You also don't have to spend hours learning about every variety of flower or cake filling. I think some women fall into beautiful internet holes and think they need to become experts on everything. I'm totally guilty of this! But if you hire professional vendors, let them be the experts. They can worry about gluten-free flour options while you binge the latest season of *Queer Eye*[10].

Finally, be yourself. Rein in your DIY ambitions unless you love crafting. Don't pressure yourself to paint three hundred glitter candles the night before a big meeting at work. Leave decor to the professionals if your seashell centerpieces are going to look like it's vodka day at preschool.

---

[8] Do you even have to ask if I did this? Of course I did this.

[9] I want these so badly. Imagine never looking like a linebacker because of under-eye mascara! #Dreamz

[10] I NEED MORE, NETFLIX!

Don't be afraid to lean on your family members and friends for help throughout your wedding planning process. Some of them might even legitimately enjoy painting glitter candles! But if your peeps don't know about weddings or seem too busy with work, grad school or raising little hellions, talk to like-minded couples online. Check out the Wedding Planning section of Reddit (lovingly nicknamed "weddit") or the forums on Wedding Wire and the Knot. You're not alone! It's comforting to discover that someone's mother-in-law is even crazier than yours.

Chapter Three

YOUR GUEST LIST

Before you start visiting venues or looking at invitations, talk to your partner about your guest list. If your parents are paying for the wedding, they may also have strong opinions about their family members, friends or coworkers who must be invited.

Francesca says that she took a lot of time narrowing down her guest list and convincing her partner that they didn't have to invite the world. "You do NOT have to invite ALL your coworkers just because you're inviting a few of them," she says. "Know where to cut so you don't need to rent out a castle to accommodate the 500 wedding guests on your initial list." Keep in mind that your guest list might also evolve, especially if you're engaged for a long period of time. You might change jobs and meet new co-workers. Your friends might also get into serious relationships.

Ah yes, those dreaded plus ones! If you've ever attended a wedding solo, you know that it can be a daunting and lonely experience – but many couples seem to forget about this as soon as they get into a relationship. Others initially plan to allow for plus-ones but, after budgeting, decide they just can't justify the additional cost. It's obviously a charitable decision to allow for all guests to have plus-ones, but if doing so costs too much, you have some other options.

One method is to allow only married guests to bring their significant others. Some couples are a bit more lenient, inviting both members of any engaged couples. Others care less about official titles and let guests bring dates or significant others if the bride and groom have personally met them before. One bride I spoke with used a different approach, inviting everyone's significant others and doling out plus-ones only if single friends wouldn't know anyone at the wedding.

For example, by this logic, if you're inviting three single people who know each other from work, you can assume they'll all hang out, so you don't need to give them plus-ones. But if you've only got one friend from the gym and you want to invite her, you should give her a plus-one because she won't know anyone else at the wedding.

I did once attend the wedding of a former co-worker who invited zero other people from our job and it was a little awkward, since I didn't have a plus-one. I sat a table with her friends from college, who were lovely as we all joined in a musical *Les Mis* flash mob[11], but the only other single person at the wedding was a guy who followed me around all night. When I know a few people at a wedding, going date-less isn't an issue, but being truly solo is hard. You might think "But my gym friend knows me," but she also knows you'll be busy and won't want to bother you. Let's be real, she might only get two minutes of face time with you.

Overall, YOU DO YOU with the plus-one situation…but as your honorary MOH, I just want to remind you to be compassionate toward your relationship-challenged friends. You want everybody to have a good time, and some people aren't adept at making conversation with strangers. Imagine if your friend said, "Hey, want to come to this work party with me? There will be free food and drinks, but I'll be off with my husband talking to everybody else the whole time and not hanging out with you. Oh, and you can't bring anyone else." Would you want to go?

Also, not everyone you invite will show up or use their plus-one. I was actually given a plus-one by a cousin but didn't bring anyone to her wedding because I was single and didn't want to open a Bumble conversation by asking someone to fly across the country and meet seven of my cousins (told you I have a lot of cousins!). So you might have more room to accommodate plus-ones than you think. You could even keep some on a secondary guest list – then when you get back an RSVP card that says no, you can offer a plus-one to a single friend. One bride I spoke with thought this was rude, but it worked for a friend of mine who had just three friends in brand new relationships. Also know that no matter how clear you are about inviting people without plus-ones, you may get "can I bring someone?" texts.

Be prepared for some drama if you cherry-pick family guests. If you invite your favorite cousin but not her brother, you might cause a rift in the family, especially when she innocently brings up the wedding and he realizes he wasn't invited. Some brides feel that you need to invite either the entire family/generation of relatives or none at all; it might depend on the size and geographic location of your family members. "People were super pissed I

---

[11] Nothing says romance like prostitutes in the French Revolution!

was having a small wedding and kept asking to be invited," says Beth from Buffalo, NY. "Sorry, but no! If I invite one aunt I have to invite them all!"

Bigger isn't always better! You might want to limit your guest list to people you're close with. "I wish I had known what a drag it would be to feel like a host on my wedding day," says Kylee from Los Angeles, CA. "I brought in so many family members I never see and felt I had to entertain. In hindsight, I would have kept it much smaller, just a small group of friends and immediate family. And I would have invested more in cocktails."

When it comes to choosing a venue with the right capacity, be prepared for all your guests to say yes – but in reality, the brides I spoke to said that only 60-75% of their guests RSVPed yes. Expect higher percentages for a local wedding with few or no out-of-town guests.

You might also find yourself in the strange position of being GLAD when guests say no because you'll save money, woo! Fewer guests also make for a more comfortable space. One bride thought her venue's capacity was 160 but later learned that this didn't really allow for a dance floor. She was relieved when 40 people RSVPed no!

Talk to your venue manager and/or wedding planner about how a group of 200 will feel in the space versus a group of 175. Ask whether a certain number of guests would require that some tables be placed on the dance floor and broken down after dinner. One bride I spoke to reduced the size of her guest list because she didn't want guests to be without a home base table later in the evening.

After you create your guest list, start compiling mailing addresses in a document. It might take a few weeks of messaging people to procure all the addresses. "One of the hardest things is getting people's up-to-date address since Ye Olde Phone Book isn't a thing anymore," says one bride. You can also use websites such as Postable to collect information.

Most couples start with "save the dates," small postcards or magnets that inform guests of your wedding date; ideally, you'll also include the wedding location and wedding website URL. Aim to send out your save the dates 8-12 months in advance so that guests don't plan conflicting vacations or their own weddings on your chosen day. If you're inviting a lot of out-of-town guests, early save the dates also enable guests to book flights at lower rates. But if your wedding guests all live in-town, you could wait a bit longer to send out STDs (insert bad Chlamydia joke here). If you've only got a handful of out-of-town guests, you could also choose to inform them of your wedding date before everyone else with a more informal method, like a text message. Finally, a reason to use all those wedding-themed emojis!!

Chapter Four

YOUR PARTNER'S INVOLVEMENT

Before you get into the nitty-gritty of "The Hokey Pokey" vs "The Cha Cha Slide,"[12] talk with your partner about the wedding elements you each care about the most. Don't agonize over six different DJ options if neither of you cares much about the DJ. Also, don't expect your partner to care about everything. Some brides I spoke to were perfectly happy with their partner's role in wedding planning, and some grooms considered themselves main planners. However, many brides told me that they were disappointed in their partner's level of involvement.

"Of course I'd love for him to have done more, but the things he was assigned to do he did," Erin explains. "Maybe not in the timeline I would have liked but he did it. The ideal would have been him volunteering or being excited to do things instead of me having to ask... but oh well."

Don't automatically think of your partner's complacency as a bad thing: maybe s/he is more excited about your life together than about one big wedding day. You can still divide up tasks (such as calling vendors for quotes) and establish deadlines so it doesn't feel like you're doing everything. If one partner has a busier job or enjoys planning, take such things into consideration.

Also, it's okay if one partner makes more choices than the other. "At first, I was annoyed that he was dragging his feet on some decisions that we needed to make," Jen says of her groom. "Once I realized that he didn't care as much

---

[12] The winner is neither. It's a lose-lose battle, people.

as I did for the majority of our wedding details, then I just took the ball and ran with it. He was so much happier for it, as was I."

"The least enjoyable part of wedding planning was all the research that goes into choosing the right vendor for everything," Jessica says. "Hours of research!" You might want to set aside specific time to work on budgeting, vendor emails, partner discussions, etc. Instead of looking at wedding stuff for a few minutes every day, you might find it more enjoyable to set aside an hour each Saturday. Make sure you still have a life!

Also, try not to let wedding planning dominate all of your time with your partner. "Sometimes the planning will be super busy and stressful, and DON'T take it out on your partner," advises a bride from New York, NY. "Enjoy time with your partner during your engagement and don't talk about the wedding at every meal or date night."

You can find lots of good vendors online, but it might be less stressful to ask your recently-married friends about vendors. "We asked friends for recommendations, and also the people in charge of events at our venue," says Erica. "The events staff at the venue had great recommendations from places to have the rehearsal dinner to florists."

Vendors can also recommend other vendors. "We found our DJ based on a referral from our photographer," says a bride from Buffalo, NY. "The photographer told us that she always dances when he DJs and that all of her brides were pleased at how easy he was to work with. I found that to be the case when we negotiated our contract. It was easier than just cold calling all of the DJs on The Knot." You don't have to get a ton of quotes for every vendor choice you make.

The most enjoyable part of wedding planning? According to many brides, it's cake! "The cake tasting was obviously bomb because it was free cake," says a bride from Los Angeles. That's right – you don't have to pay to taste multiple kinds of cake at a bakery. Why am I not pretending to get married and eating free cake all the damn time? If your partner enjoys cake, this is a part of the process that you might actually get him or her to participate in and enjoy.

If you can't agree on a cake, you might consider having a smaller, secondary cake – often called a groom's cake – in addition to a main cake. This can be a good option if your partner insists on having a *Jurassic Park*-themed cake[13]. You can also serve cupcakes.

"I loved coming up with DIY elements that made sense for us," says Kristin. Our place cards were in little matchbox cars (he's a mechanic, I love *The Fast and the Furious*), and we made our own corn hole boards and card box. We also made all the elements for the cupcakes to sit on."

---

[13] Yes, I've actually been to a wedding that featured a Jurassic Park cake. RAWR. (Wait, did dinos roar?)

Unfortunately, not every wedding planning task will be a blast – and it can be frustrating if a partner won't do what was promised or procrastinates so much that it stresses you out or makes you feel like you have to nag[14]. But to save yourself some aggravation, first, make sure your partner knows what's important to you and what you expect him or her to do. Some people just need very clear directions and are happy to follow them. Maybe your partner says "I don't care" or "Whatever you want," thinking this sounds flexible and helpful, but all you really want is a firm YES/NO or an "I like the black better than the silver." Just explain that to him or her.

"Communication is so important," says one Los Angeles bride, who found that the wedding planning discussions she had with her partner were a window into what her marriage would be like. She recommends positive reinforcement, which she admits she learned about from her dog trainer. "It works for everything!" she says, both laughing and serious. Instead of chastising your partner for what he or she has done wrong, talk about what you would like him or her to do. Then, express your satisfaction when he or she does these things.

You might also try explaining to your partner that a lot of emotional labor goes into planning a wedding (especially when you have a full-time job of your own). But it's tricky – he or she may take it as a personal attack. S/he may say, "I don't even want a wedding! Let's just go to the courthouse!" To which you can respond, "We've already spent fifteen grand on goddamn gourmet donuts and the jazz-fusion band your father demanded."

"Walking that fine line to keep the peace and not upset your partner is something women are taught to accept as their duty from an early age," writes Gemma Hartley in *Harper's Bazaar*. "It's frustrating to be saddled with all of these responsibilities, no one to acknowledge the work you are doing, and no way to change it without a major confrontation."[15]

After talking to numerous brides, here is the best advice I can offer about managing your partner's role in the process: in general, choose a life partner who listens and who gives a shit if you are upset about something. When it comes to your wedding, don't expect your partner to care about all the details. Instead of trying to make him or her care about details, take the steps that will make YOU less upset or stressed out about the fact that he or she doesn't care. "The details of the wedding aren't as important as the way you feel about the person you're marrying," says Emily.

---

[14] Don't you love the term "nag"? You wouldn't have to nag if they fucking did what they promised they were going to do, right?

[15] Hartley, Gemma. "Women Aren't Nags—We're Just Fed Up." *Harper's Bazaar.* 27 September 2017.
https://www.harpersbazaar.com/culture/features/a12063822/emotional-labor-gender-equality/

Besides, a super-involved partner might not be as amazing as you might think. "I found it to be a bit annoying!" says Anastasiya. "I love that he took some of the pressure off decision making, but he definitely forced me to budget certain things."

Also, therapy or counseling can be helpful. One bride told me she didn't do any premarital counseling and wished she had.

"It was massively helpful in figuring out why fights just drag out," says David from Beaverton, OR. "I think we did four sessions."

Adds Sean from Santa Barbara, CA: "We had done counseling as part of improving our relationship, not as any part of the engagement or wedding. In fact, our therapist was our officiant, so that should give you an indication of how we felt about it."

On the other hand, some couples disliked church-required counseling. "[I] felt it was a waste of time unless you're 18 and not very mature," says a bride from New Orleans, LA. "It was very obvious to me, with the topics like 'Have you talked about having kids?'"

Chapter Five

WEDDING PLANNERS AND COORDINATORS

Nothing is more controversial than the question of whether you need a wedding planner!

"Do everything yourself if you can!" says the Amherst bride. "No one else knows you as a couple or your style as well as you do."

But Kristin disagrees: "I hired a planner right away and knew it would be great, but I had no idea how much it would help," she says. "She was worth her weight in gold."

First, let's make an important distinction:

WEDDING PLANNERS assist you through the entire year-long process of wedding planning. They can suggest options, make calls, go over contracts and provide helpful documents. They also execute your plans (often with the help of an assistant or two) on your wedding day.

WEDDING COORDINATORS show up on the day of your wedding and execute the plans that you have made yourself. They might be called day-of coordinators or month-of coordinators depending on how early they get in touch before your wedding to organize and finalize plans. Some wedding venues also provide you with a coordinator, and some places REQUIRE you to use this person.

Explains Francesca: "The venue provided a Maître D and a bridal attendant to service all my needs. Yay! Thanks. Oh, I need to tip them $150 each?! For what? She followed me around asking if I needed anything all night. But I didn't. I guess if I'd needed her, it would have been worth it."

On the other hand, Anastasiya liked her venue's coordinator. "We had a wedding day-of coordinator who came with the venue, which was awesome," she says.

"If you are not organized or have trouble making decisions, a wedding planner would be helpful," says Jessica. "I'm extremely organized and self-sufficient, so I used The Knot to help me stay focused, but did everything myself (with the help of my husband)."

"I felt stressed and overwhelmed making decisions so it would have been nice to have a wedding planner to make decisions for me," says Alissa.

"I recommend a full wedding planner if you can afford it," says a Los Angeles bride who was disappointed with her "somewhere in-between" coordinator (i.e. the person wasn't a full wedding planner but did more and charged more than a typical coordinator). "The first part of the process ended up being frustrating, as she didn't respond to emails right away, and I basically planned a lot of it myself anyway."

Here's how I can make sense of the conflicting advice: if you are an organized control freak who likes making spreadsheets and needs to comb over every contract detail yourself, then you don't need a planner because you'll just be paying someone to do the work you're already doing.

"Sometimes they can negotiate better rates with preferred vendors but not enough to offset the costs," adds Carolyn from New York, NY.

But if you hate planning and can afford the cost, a wedding planner might improve your experience. "They are worth every penny," says one Los Angeles bride. "If you can't afford it, a coordinator is the next best thing."

In fact, almost everyone told me that a day-of coordinator is essential. When vendors show up at your wedding, they're going to have questions. When problems arise, they're going to need solutions. If you don't have a coordinator, YOU are the person who will need to take care of all this – and that might be stressful. Also, because brides tend to do the bulk of the wedding planning, vendors usually contact brides before grooms. Yay traditional gender roles!

"I absolutely recommend a day-of coordinator," says another Los Angeles bride. "You don't want to be handing out final bills and tips to people and putting out fires on the day of your wedding."

Another agrees: "Let someone else worry about stuff on the day!"

If you use a coordinator, s/he can be the point-person as vendors arrive while you're chugging mimosas and getting your hair done. If you're a budget-first person and you don't mind being the point person, then skip the coordinator. One of my friends did this successfully, but it was also her problem when the beverage store said they had no record of her wine and beer order – on the morning of her wedding! Because she was dealing with this, she didn't have time to do as many pre-wedding photos as she wanted.

Another bride told me that it was her coordinator who realized they'd need to arrange for a shaded tent so that her pies wouldn't melt during a surprise heat wave. Coordinators can solve problems you'd never be able to predict on your own.

Also, be honest with yourself about your skill set. "Women tell me that they want their wedding to be the best day of their lives," says Gina, a wedding coordinator who has worked both lavish hotel weddings and rustic campsite nuptials across California and Washington. "But if you've never even thrown a dinner party where you had to make the garlic bread and lasagna both ready at the right time, how are you going to coordinate a flawless 200-person event?"

"Everyone, and I mean everyone, no matter how organized they are, should have a day-of coordinator," says Jamie from Los Angeles, CA. "A good day-of coordinator really coordinates the week of the wedding and helps your vision come to life so you can just enjoy the day. I do events for a living and am completely comfortable organizing everything, and I am still so thankful for my day-of coordinator."

Jen agrees: "My coordinator was great and put my plan for the day in motion. She kept us as close to the schedule as possible so I didn't have to stress about the time at all. She took care of so many things that I didn't even know about until after the wedding, like when my friend's heel broke and she fixed it with tape. And the cake delivery person had a problem finding the venue, but she got it there and decorated."

When choosing a coordinator, remember that this person will have to deal with all your other vendors. One bride told me that a catering meeting turned into a tense argument between the coordinator and the catering manager, who didn't get along. Meanwhile, a groom said that vendors would email him and his wife to complain about their coordinator! You may want to find out which coordinators and vendors have had positive experiences with each other in the past before you make your selections.

If you don't have a planner or coordinator, remember that you will need to be in contact with – and stay on top of – multiple vendors.

"The only issue we had was with the photographer, who stopped returning phone calls or emails," Erica says. "At one point we weren't sure she would show up. As it turned out, her husband filed for divorce the morning of our wedding (which she told us upon her arrival), so she was going through a tough time. We ended up fighting with her for part of our money back, because we didn't end up getting half the things we paid for (pre-wedding meeting to discuss desired shots, posting our pictures on her website so people could view and order shots, post-wedding session which we'd paid for in advance, etc.). Luckily, she was very talented, and the pictures she did take turned out great."

At the very least, you can appoint your Maid of Honor, Best Man, parent or friend to be the point-person for vendor logistics on the day of the wedding, especially if they've recently gotten married or if they're someone who works in events. You can also write up a specific plan/itinerary and delegate various duties to different people. Maybe a Best Man or Maid of Honor can coordinate food and beverage vendors while your mom takes care of décor setup, for example.

"I don't think a wedding planner is necessary, but I highly recommend letting a couple key friends in on the details so they can help direct," says Lauren from West Seneca, NY. "I also wrote up itineraries of who had to be where, when and doing what for all the people in the wedding party. That was a huge win."

Even if you have a planner or coordinator, you might want to do this anyway. At a friend's wedding, the coordinator didn't send us a timeline or tell us the order of the speeches. I was never sure if it was a good time to shove chicken in my mouth or if I'd need to stand up and speak.

Kait has just one word of advice for brides: "Spreadsheet."

●

Chapter Six

YOUR WEDDING PLANNING TIMELINE

Below is a sample timeline with all the major things you'll need to do to plan your wedding. Keep in mind that it's common to be working on many items on this list at the same time as you research vendors, wait for quotes, schedule meetings, etc. Also, many of these things are optional – YOU DO YOU!

When in doubt, give yourself extra time for troubleshooting in case vendors fall through or items arrive busted (literally or figuratively). That said, don't worry if you're behind on some of these benchmarks – they're all approximate. You WILL end up hitched!

12 months away	Make a guest list.
	Look at venues based on your approximate total number of guests.
	Ask your loved ones to be in your bridal party, and find out if they're already booked on certain dates (we all have a YEAR OF THE WEDDINGS).
	Lock in venue and date.
11 months away	Get engagement photos taken. Sooner is better if you want to put them on save the dates.
	When your photos come back, get save the dates printed (or create electronic versions); you can also get save the dates without photos. Order a few extra just in case.

	If you have out-of-town guests, secure hotel blocks.
	Create a wedding website with some basic content: your names, your wedding date and your wedding city.
	Send out save the dates.
	Create a wedding registry and put a few items on it if relatives ask about engagement gifts. Begin keeping a document of who sends what so you can send thank you notes later.
	Ask your parents if they plan to contribute anything to the wedding budget.
	Establish your wedding budget. Some couples do this before looking at venues, but you may need to see venue proposals with costs based on guest count before you establish your complete budget. Include gratuities.
	Get savings plan in place if you don't already have enough cold, hard cash.
	Hire wedding planner or wedding coordinator.
10 months away	Begin shopping for wedding dress.
9 months away	Order wedding dress if you're getting one made-to-order through a traditional bridal salon.
	Hire photographer and videographer.
	Secure catering and bar.
	Rent tables, chairs, linens, etc. if you're not getting them through your caterer or venue.
	Hire band, DJ, string quartet, or any other performers.
	Secure photo booth, fireworks or any other guest entertainment.
8 months away	Hire officiant.
	Hire and schedule trials with makeup artist and hairstylist.

7 months away	Talk to your friends/bridal party about bachelor and bachelorette parties (if everybody's local, you can wait longer).
	Hire florist.
	Schedule cake tastings.
6 months away	Secure limos and shuttles.
	Begin arranging rehearsal dinner, larger welcome dinner and/or farewell brunch.
	Decide on cake.
	Purchase alcohol and design signature cocktails.
	Order invitations.
	Finish filling in details on wedding website.
	Plan honeymoon.
	Start shopping for bridesmaid dresses and suits/tuxedos.
5 months away	Finish putting items on wedding registry.
	Order bridesmaid dresses and suits/tuxedos.
	Purchase veil.
	Purchase outfits for moms, flower girl, ring bearer, etc.
4 months away	Finalize rehearsal dinner (or begin to plan it if it's small).
	Order wedding rings.
3 months away	Send out invitations.
	Schedule bridal gown fittings or purchase non-custom gown.
	Purchase and finalize décor, guestbook, cake topper, etc.
	Adjust your birth control schedule so you don't get your period on your wedding day. Yay womanhood!
2 months away	Tell people you'd like them to give speeches.
	Order place cards, menus and ceremony programs.
	Purchase shoes, jewelry and any other accessories.
	Schedule haircut appointments, manicures, facials, etc.

	Plan any beauty regimens – teeth whitening, hair dye, etc.
	Get lit at your bachelor/bachelorette party!
1 month away	Purchase bridal party gifts.
	Chase down anyone who hasn't RSVPed.
	Check your wedding registry and add more things if you need to.
	Obtain a marriage license, following any state-specific time regulations. Decide if you're changing your name so you don't have to file more paperwork later.
2 weeks away	Write vows.
	Give caterer the final guest count.
	Give venue manager a list of vendor requests.
	Give coordinators, appointed friends/relatives and bridal party members the wedding day schedule, responsibilities and vendor info, including phone numbers.
	Confirm everything – delivery times, locations, etc. – with each vendor. Give vendors someone to call with day-of questions or emergencies.
FINAL WEEK	Deliver welcome baskets to out-of-town hotel guests.
	Deliver décor items to coordinator or venue manager.
	Give marriage license to officiant.
	Write a card or letter for your love to read on the day.
	Freak out because you're a human and IT'S OKAY TO HAVE EMOTIONS!
WEDDING WEEKEND	Pack everything you'll need for your wedding, wedding night and honeymoon.
	Give gifts to relatives and bridal party members at the rehearsal dinner.
	Give wedding bands to the Best Man or other appointed person to hold during the ceremony.

	Give appointed friends/family members final payment envelopes to be given to vendors on the wedding day.
WEDDING DAY	HAVE AN AMAZING TIME!
REST OF YOUR LIFE	GO ON YOUR BADASS HONEYMOON!
	OH MY GOD CAN YOU BELIEVE THERE ARE THIS MANY THINGS?
	Unwrap gifts and write thank-you notes.
	Get your photos/videos back and bask in how happy and hot you look.
	Be married ☺
ONE YEAR LATER	Eat the piece of wedding cake that you put in the freezer and somehow haven't scarfed yet!

Chapter Seven

YOUR VENUE, CEREMONY AND VOWS

When I was a wee kiddo, I found wedding ceremonies so BORING. And to be fair, I still find them severely lacking in cake. But your wedding ceremony is the actual point of your wedding. You'll profess your love and commitment to your partner, in front of all your friends, family members and work besties. In our garbage fire of a world, we probably need a few more sincere professions of love and commitment! Maybe you should get married twice, just to send more good vibes into the universe.

You can get married almost anywhere: a church, a courthouse, a public beach, a garden, a park, a hotel ballroom, a museum, a campground, a backyard, a living room or even in virtual reality[16].

Alissa says that her favorite part of planning was walking into her venue and knowing it was the place she wanted. "I'm not really the girl who dreamed about my wedding as a little girl, but picking the venue I thought was beautiful did make it feel kind of like a fairy tale," she says.

You might want to visit venues and ask what dates they have available instead of choosing the date first and then finding a venue available on that particular date. You might discover that everywhere in your area is booked, which could be a pain if you've already told everyone your date. Also think about weather (if outdoors), sports schedules and your job schedule when choosing your venue and date.

Remember that venues not designed for weddings will require more work, planning and possibly money. Gina says not to underestimate the fact that

---

[16] Rubin, Peter. "What a Real Wedding in a Virtual Reality Space Says About the Future." *Wired.* April 2018. https://www.wired.com/story/virtual-reality-wedding/

hotel and banquet hall employees do weddings all the time and know exactly what to do.

Also think about your guests' physical comfort. Remember that the woods means bugs! You might want to provide bug spray or incorporate citronella candles into your décor. In the summer heat, consider providing shade, sunglasses, parasols, fans and/or water. You can also try to schedule the time of your ceremony based on when the sun is high or low in the sky. If it's cold or rainy, offer blankets or pashminas, or bring the fun indoors. If your venue is so rustic that it doesn't have heat and/or air conditioning[17], please schedule carefully and maybe even find a new venue. Remember that men will be dressed warmly, women might have bare shoulders and open-toed shoes, and not all guests can handle the elements as well as your badass self can. "I always tell brides to think about the youngest and the oldest person who will be invited," says Gina.

When you find yourself thinking, "THE GUESTS MUST SUFFER FOR MY VISION," it's time to steer the ship back to reality.

Consider how far guests will have to walk from parking/shuttle areas. For long distances or uneven terrain, you might want to advise guests on appropriate footwear. Choose your spaces carefully; dramatic cliffs can make for great wedding photos, but they can be a challenge for grandmas and people with mobility issues. Maybe the cliff would be a better choice for your engagement photo session. Also, vendors will have to carry equipment from parking areas to ceremony spaces. Don't kill your DJ.

Many couples have their ceremonies and receptions in the same place to make everything easier for planning and for guests, but a church wedding means that you'll need a separate reception space. Think about whether you want guests to have to transport themselves from the ceremony space to the reception space or if you'd like to provide a shuttle.

You generally have two options for your ceremony/reception timeline: either you'll do the ceremony, then pictures, then the reception, or you'll do a "first look" and pictures, then the reception immediately after. The first option allows you to see your partner for the first time as you're walking down the aisle, if that's important to you. Keep in mind, though, that your coordinator and photographer can make sure a first look is still special; many couples have told me that walking down the aisle is still very moving even when you've already seen your betrothed in their gown/tux.

"I think I would have been an emotional mess walking down the aisle if I didn't do a first look," says a Los Angeles bride. In fact, many brides found that doing a first look reduced ceremony stress.

If you're worried about ugly-crying when you walk down the aisle or say your vows, first remember that it's okay to have emotions. EMOTIONS

---

[17] This is a thing! Read fine print!

ARE NATURAL AND GOOD! If we taught boys and men that they shouldn't repress their emotions, maybe toxic masculinity wouldn't be such a thing. Besides, anyone who doesn't tear up on their wedding day might be an alien sent to Earth for reconnaissance or a more sinister mission, like tricking a human into falling in love![18] That said, I understand that you don't want your face to look like a river of mascara when you're five minutes into an 8-hour wedding. Here's a strategy I read somewhere that has actually worked for me (albeit during non-wedding scenarios): instead of thinking "Don't cry, don't cry," tell yourself, "I will cry. I will cry." Somehow, it's calming. Instead of fighting your emotions and showing that conflict on your face, submit to your emotions – and you might actually cry less. You can also focus on breathing deeply, and make sure someone nearby has some tissues!

Having attended some church ceremonies with pictures afterward, I will say that it's a little awkward, as a guest, to attend a wedding ceremony, return to your hotel for a couple hours and then head back out for the reception. You don't really know what to do with yourself, and you kinda want to eat but don't want to spoil your appetite. My family's solution is generally to eat as much as possible and add melted mozzarella, but I admittedly prefer weddings with receptions directly after the ceremony. If you have a wedding planner, talk to her/him about your options. Logistics might determine your timeline – what the church requires, when the sun is setting, how many hours you want to pay vendors for, etc.

DO NOT HALF-ASS YOUR RAIN PLAN. I'll say it again: DO NOT HALF-ASS YOUR RAIN PLAN. I really hope that you get the best possible weather for your wedding day – but you may not get dry sunshine. You know where you live. You know what month it is. Don't be in denial like Jenny McCarthy on vaccination day. Talk to your venue coordinator about what will happen if it rains (or is very cold). Make sure you are happy with what your wedding will look like if you have to do all of it indoors, under a tent, etc. If you would be unhappy with the required rain-plan arrangement, then pick a new venue.

When it comes to the ceremony, guests tend to look for two things: personality and brevity. If your ceremony is religious, you may not have a choice in ceremony length – but resist the urge to add extra readings or musical performances if your ceremony is already on the long side. Also, try to stick to your schedule.

The outdoors are lovely, but it is completely fine to get married indoors! It's a lot easier to control an indoor environment. Your guests will sweat a normal amount, and your hair won't look like Bridget Jones' frizzy disaster after she gets out of the convertible with stupid Daniel. You also won't run

---

[18] If you see something, say something!

the risk of a public beach rando drowning out your expensive string quartet with his drum circle.

When considering a venue, think about where you'll put everything. Is there enough room for a live band AND a photo booth? Is there a bridal suite where you can get ready? (If not, make a plan for where you'll get ready and how you'll get to the venue.) Is there a secure room where you can store valuables and cards? Coordinators have warned me that guests or passers-by may try to steal cards or gifts.

Ceremonies only need to be as formal as you want them to be. David says that the best part of his wedding was a nod to *Doctor Who*. "Our officiant dressed as the fourth Doctor, pulling out a blue Tardis book with his notes and speeches," he says.

In fact, many wedding guests told me that they hate wedding ceremonies that are overly long, formal or traditional. Sean also says he dislikes when a couple doesn't make it their own. "There are no rules, do whatever the hell you want," he says.

"I really like meaningful ceremonies," says a bride from Seattle, WA. "They don't have to be serious or long but should reflect the couple and feel like the transition that it is. I dislike the format of the standard timeline and predictability of how a wedding day should go. Change it around."

David says he likes "humor" the most at weddings. "A sense of who they are. People not taking things too seriously. It's a party, after all."

Many brides and grooms struggle with how much religion to include in their ceremonies. Your parents may have a lot of opinions about this.

"For our wedding ceremony, our biggest concern was for it to be short," says Jen. "My husband and I discussed it, and although he grew up with a more religious background, we decided the people we are now aren't tied to a traditional religion. We kept it more focused on love. His parents would have loved to have it be religious. It was a sore subject for a moment, but they were able to move past it. Our parents really wanted us to do what we both wanted."

"The decision to have a religious ceremony was mostly us, although each of our parents had a couple of specific requests," Sam says. "That said, we weren't always sure we wanted a Jewish ceremony. At first we were a little nervous about it, because we worried our ceremony might feel impersonal and cookie-cutter. But as we looked into planning a Jewish ceremony, we became more and more excited about it."

"We're both moderately religious reform Jews, but we were also both sort of lapsed Jews," Sam continues. "We'd had trouble as adults finding a Jewish community that we connected with. And so part of our reluctance was also this idea that we might be 'faking it'. We didn't want to be people who had a religious wedding because we were supposed to or because our parents expected it. It seemed like it could end up being inauthentic. We wanted to make sure that we felt personally connected to all of the rituals in the ceremony."

Ultimately, he advises couples to "focus on the reasons you want to have a religious wedding and make sure you're accomplishing those."

"For us, it was connecting with traditions that were thousands of years old, that had been the same for our parents and grandparents," he says. "So the parts we chose to use, we more or less did with no alteration. We ended up ADDING things more than changing or cutting things."

Sam also says that the book *The Jewish Wedding Now* by Anita Diamant was a big help.

You might also consider mixing some religious elements with readings from literature. I've been to weddings that included both bible verses and Shakespeare sonnets; passages from novels can also be romantic. You could even throw in quotes from movies such as *The Princess Bride*. Readings are a fun way to involve friends and family members who aren't in your wedding party. Just pick people who can enunciate and project well!

Some old traditions might make you a little uncomfortable, like the vow to "love, honor and obey" your husband. Gross! But you don't have to include that vow or any other outdated tradition. In fact, your ceremony can be a celebration of equality as much as love. You do you!

If you've always imagined having your father walking you down the aisle, go for it! But if you don't like this idea or don't have a father figure in your life, you have options. Many brides have both parents walk them down the aisle, or just a mom, a sibling, a child or some other important person in their life. Brides can have their fathers give them away, or, when your officiant asks "Who gives this woman," he can say "Her mother and I do," or both the father AND mother can come up to the officiant and say "We do." You could also have your mom give you away, or skip the whole "giving away" thing. YOU ARE A MODERN WOMAN AND NOBODY OWNS YOU.

For a marriage to be legally binding, your wedding ceremony needs to include a declaration of intent (the "I do" moment) and a pronouncement (the "I now pronounce you" moment. Most ceremonies also contain an introduction, some readings and some music – but these two elements are the only absolutely required parts.

You and your partner should talk to your officiant about the order of the ceremony as well as your desired tone. You'll want a stranger to get to know you a little so that the ceremony is personal. With a friend or relative, this isn't a problem – but you might have to teach your friend or relative about how to be effective and satisfy your expectations. Are you cool with improvisation, or do you want everything perfectly planned out? You want your officiant to take charge of the moment so that you can enjoy the ceremony and focus on your vows. Choose someone who makes that easy! I'd also avoid picking an officiant who might tell inappropriate stories, make the ceremony about him/herself, go on and on, forget something, or break down into tears.

An experienced officiant can walk you through the usual ceremony elements and tailor what they say to you. If you don't want language about "obeying" your spouse or "til death to us part," say so. One perk of using a friend as an officiant is that you might avoid awkward mistakes. The priest at my cousin's wedding called her by the wrong name! Luckily, she found it funny; I would have smashed some Communion wafers.

You might also want to give your officiant a specific book or binder to read from. "I am so sick of seeing people read off of their iPhones at formal events," says a bride from Buffalo, NY. This goes for vows, too – if you're writing original vows, talk to your partner about what you'll be reading them from. I'm not saying you need to drop $50 on a vow book you'll never use again – but whatever you hold will be in your photos forever. It could also serve as a meaningful keepsake, if you're into such things.

Also, make sure your officiant gets ordained (more on this in Chapter Twenty-Four) and knows to file your marriage license after your wedding. Many officiants get ordained online, but a handful of locales only allow marriages by officiants who've attended seminary or obtained a theology degree. Do some research before you lock in your officiant.

Tradition dictates that the bride's guests should sit on the left, while the groom's guests should sit on the right. (This is flipped in traditional Jewish ceremonies.) Some couples have the bride and groom stay on the side of their respective guests, but you can switch this up if you want to give each person's guests the best view of their facial expressions during the ceremony. It's up to you if you want to designate ushers to guide guests to a particular side (many couples today let guests sit anywhere). If you do use ushers, seats should be filled from the front to the back, leaving any special VIP seats reserved. Consider asking your most attractive friends to be ushers; nothing sexes up a ceremony like a hot usher.

Some couples pair up bridesmaids and groomsmen to walk down the aisle, while others have the groomsmen stand at the front of the aisle while just the bridesmaids and Maid of Honor do the walking.

Flower girls and ring bearers are optional, and you can also choose bubbles over flowers or have ring bearers carry signs instead of rings (do you really want to trust a two year-old with actual gold?). I've also heard of an older ring bearer pulling a younger flower girl in a wagon – adorable! If you decide to involve young children in your ceremony, go over their responsibilities RIGHT before the wedding and make sure their parents are nearby to corral them. You might even have a young flower girl's mom walk her all the way down the aisle. You could also consider letting boys distribute flowers or letting girls handle rings. SCREW THOSE GENDER ROLES!

Be cool with the fact that toddlers of all genders will have no idea what the hell is going on. They will likely not follow directions and might get stage fright at the last minute or straight-up refuse to participate, simply because toddlers are adorable little asshole dictators. At my preschool graduation, I smiled for tons of photos in my homemade Styrofoam plate hat but then refused to wear it, sing songs or do hand motions at the actual ceremony[19].

At my best friend's wedding, the flower girls didn't actually spread any flower petals until the very end of the aisle, and then both the flower girls and the ring bearers ran around picking up petals for the entire ceremony. We all found it cute and hilarious – but if this would bother you, consider leaving little kids out of the ceremony.

Kids can definitely create unexpected memories, though. "My two year-old niece shouted 'penis!' during the ceremony, but that was the best thing to happen," says Kristin.

One of the more enjoyable – or perhaps agonizing – parts of wedding planning is choosing a song for you to walk down the aisle to (the "processional") and the song for you to leave the ceremony to, right after you're pronounced married (the "recessional"). Whether you like modern pop songs, classic love songs or traditional, classical music, the options are endless. I've even been to a wedding that ended with the *Star Wars* theme song. Just make sure your DJ or coordinator knows when to cue the song. For the recessional, a good, clear cue is for the bride and groom to raise their held hands in a kind of victory gesture. You'll also want to pick a fun song for when you and your bridal party are introduced as you all enter the reception.

CUTE ROMANCE ALERT: More than one groom told me that the vows were one of the best parts of the wedding day. "We had tunnel vision the entire time," Sean says. "No one else existed in the world."

Many couples write their vows the week of their wedding – but leave some time to talk to your partner about what you expect. If you're writing your own vows, agree on an approximate word count. I once attended a wedding ceremony where the bride wrote beautiful, specific vows that lasted at least a minute, and the groom responded with a heartfelt but painfully short sentence. Awkward! Also, talk with your partner about how formal or informal you'd like the vows to be. Many couples do a mix of traditional and modern vows – it just depends on your personality. If you're getting married in a church, you might be required to stick with formal, standard vows. But even if you're not, it's okay to use standard vows. If you're not good at public speaking or creative writing, or if you're worried you're going to be an emotional mess, standard vows might be the right choice for you.

---

[19] I'd like to think that I refused the indignity of this hat because, at this very moment, I developed a super sophisticated fashion sense.

Even if you memorize your non-standard vows, have a copy in front of you so you won't be worried about forgetting something during such an intense, emotional moment.

If you're writing your vows, have a close friend or family member read over them before you write a final draft. In your vows, you can lightly tease your partner about something, like how you vow not to get mad when they take forever to choose a restaurant, but try not to make your vows negative or critical – if anything, it'd be the time to lightly tease yourself instead. Vows are also not a good time to tell inappropriate stories – keep things PG. If you know you're good at humor, you can throw in some jokes (one writer I know started his vows with "Thanks for coming tonight," which I've always loved), but overall, your vows should be more about heartfelt promises than a comedy performance.

If you write for a living, the pressure to be both moving and hilarious can be enormous. "What if I bombed at my own wedding?" asks comedy writer Josh Gondelman in *The New York Times*. But "this wasn't a crowd that needed me to kill," he writes. "What this event called for was earnestness."[20]

Indeed, Owen Wilson's advice to Rachel McAdams in *Wedding Crashers* is pretty solid: "People want something from the heart."

---

[20] Gondelman, Josh. "What if I Bombed at My Own Wedding?" *The New York Times*. 1 Sept 2017.
https://www.nytimes.com/2017/09/01/opinion/sunday/what-if-i-bombed-at-my-own-wedding.html

Chapter Eight

YOUR KICKASS RECEPTION

A common refrain from brides and grooms is "I just want my guests to have a good time."

Congrats, you're not a monster!!

If you've attended many weddings, you probably already have a list of things that annoy and excite you. What are other people's weddings if not useful research trips? Okay, FINE, they're celebrations of love, but they're also a chance to pretend you're on that old TLC show *Four Weddings* as you judge overcooked chicken and hairy relatives who inexplicably disrobe on the dance floor.

On the off chance you haven't yet gone pro on the wedding guest circuit, here are some tips for making sure everybody has a rockin' time at your reception.

Pick music that will appeal to everyone. Says a bride from New Orleans, LA: "There is such a thing as too many line dance songs in a row."

Food is also a big priority for guests. Many brides and grooms ultimately have to choose catering options that fit in their budget and will please the most guests (hence boring chicken and veggies). But staying in budget doesn't mean you can't be creative. I've eaten both Vietnamese and Southern BBQ at budget-conscious weddings and enjoyed both immensely. If you're thinking of doing something unique, go for it!

I have also enjoyed both plated and buffet meals, but you should keep a few things in mind if you opt for a buffet.

"I originally thought a buffet would be cool," says Lauren, a fellow wedding guest pro who attended a beautiful wedding in the mountains of Colorado. "But all the good stuff ran out early, so when we got called to go, we didn't get any French fries or burgers. We were stuck with the salad and after dinner, we were still hungry." Perhaps the caterer under-estimated the amount of food they'd need; Lauren also says that some guests took seconds before her table got their first portions, so perhaps the food shortage was the fault of a wedding coordinator.

"With a plated meal, everyone gets their own dish," she says.

I've always thought it would be fun to feature food stations of multiple cuisines to showcase the diversity of my city's food, but an older wedding guest told me she didn't enjoy a wedding that was set up this way.

"Since everybody was up going from station to station, it felt like you never got to talk to the people at your table," she says.

After dinner, you might avoid making guests participate in too many strictly scheduled moments. "I've enjoyed weddings that were designed to feel casual and fun, like a joyful get-together," says a groom from New Mexico. "I dislike weddings that feel very strict and formal, like someone is herding everyone around to make sure the trains run on time."

If this resonates with you, you might also avoid a send-off (also known as a farewell or sparkler farewell) at the end of the night. For a send-off, all the guests form two lines, and you and your partner walk through the crowd on your way to a car that will take you to your hotel. Some couples also give guests sparklers, bubbles or confetti to hold as they pass through. These moments make for amazing photos, but herding 150 drunk people into a send-off line takes time. (It might also take a while for you and your partner to round up all the items you need to take with you to the hotel. Do you even know where your phone is?) The guests who follow directions and stand in the right spot early on may get bored.

Also, if a lot of guests are still around for your send-off line, it means that you're basically the first people to leave the wedding. Is that what you want? You're spending so much that you probably don't want to cut things short. But if you wait until most people are gone, then the line might be kind of small. Finally, I wouldn't do a send-off unless you have a wedding planner/coordinator to handle it for you.

Don't skimp on alcohol at your reception. The bar is what will ensure many guests will have a good time, and it's also what inspires people to get up and dance[21]. I do still maintain that it's fine to serve just beer and wine – or beer, wine and one or two signature cocktails – but don't underestimate how much your guests can drink over the course of five hours. A bartender who says "We're out of Prosecco" quickly becomes my enemy. The common

---

[21] At her wedding, my best friend put a sign on the bar that said "You can dance!" – Vodka, which I loved. If people don't dance, you can also be like my cousin, who stole the mic, squatted in the middle of the dance floor and yelled, "THIS IS MY WEDDING! GET ON THE DANCE FLOOR!" until guests complied. She claims not to remember this.

rule of thumb is to plan for each guest to consume two drinks during cocktail hour and one drink per hour every hour after that.

Many couples save money by closing the bar during dinner or transition periods between cocktail hour and dinner; this will also ensure that guests won't be walking around while people are giving toasts and speeches. However, I have observed guests get upset when they couldn't get a drink and the wait staff who bring wine to each table were nowhere to be found. Guests also get cranky when they have to wait in long lines for drinks at cocktail hour, so make sure you have enough bartenders. Servers can also carry trays of pre-poured champagne, wine or signature cocktails during cocktail hour so that lines don't get too long. Choosing a signature cocktail that is quick to mix might also help.

As important as alcohol is to many guests, don't forget to have some kind of non-alcoholic option, like sparkling water, soda or juice. If you're stocking the bar with liquor, you'll probably get these as mixers. But if you're only serving beer and wine, don't forget about your pregnant, teenage and non-lush friends.

Many couples today skip the bouquet toss. In this classic reception moment, the DJ will call all non-married women out onto the dance floor, and the bride will chuck her bouquet into them while facing away from this festering plague of spinster-dom. Legend has it that the woman lucky enough to catch the blooms will be next to marry. The bouquet toss can be a cute but also outdated practice, and many single women feel embarrassed to be paraded out on the dance floor like this. One bride I know put a spin on the tradition by turning around and then handing out single, long-stemmed red roses to all of her single friends, which I thought was cute. You are certainly welcome to stick to the traditional way, but it might also be fun to get creative. Maybe force single men to come out too? Maybe throw cash? Ain't nobody too embarrassed of being single to grab some stray Hamiltons. Just know that you don't HAVE to include a bouquet toss just because some blog put it on a list.

Even weirder than the bouquet toss is the garter toss. Traditionally, after the bouquet toss, the bride will sit on a chair in the middle of the dance floor while the groom slides his hand up her dress – or uses his teeth! – to take a large, shiny scrunchie off her thigh. (Apparently, back in the day, the garter was made of a piece of the bride's dress and symbolized good luck.) The groom then throws the garter into a crowd of single men, and the recipient gets to place the garter on the leg of the woman who won the bouquet toss. WTF, right? I don't want to be a killjoy here, but do you really want to force two of your guests – who might be complete strangers – to do this in front of your whole reception? Maybe you should rig the contest ahead of time and let two friends do a fun performance. Or you could instruct the woman to kick the man while he's under her skirt as some cool anti-patriarchy performance art. One of your guests is bound to be a trained medical professional who can help if she goes too far, right?

If you like the idea of wearing a garter – you can get a monogrammed one or even a Batman one because Weddings + Internet + Capitalism is a magical combo – keep in mind you can also do so without the toss.

If a lot of kids will be attending your reception, consider creating an area with toys and games. You could also ban children completely. This can be a controversial topic – you're inviting people to a family event, but then banning family members and asking them to pay for babysitters – but sometimes even parents would like to attend an adults-only event. There's no right or wrong answer to this; you do you. I have been to lovely adults-only weddings and lovely kid-friendly weddings. You can also invite only the children of your bridal party members or only the children who are participating in the wedding ceremony.

Guests enjoy having options for activities at a wedding. Photo booths, party games (like horseshoes, croquet or corn-hole), live animal photo-ops, fireworks, karaoke, ice cream carts, dessert bars and late-night snacks give guests alternatives to dancing – or things they can do while on restorative breaks between "Cotton Eyed Joe" and "Baby Got Back." Signing the guestbook and looking at family photos can also occupy guests. Don't assume that people are having a bad time if they aren't five-hour dancing machines!

But some people LOVE shakin' it – and I was surprised by how many women at my best friend's wedding made use of the bright palm tree flip flops she put out in a metal tin with a cute "Put On Some Dancing Shoes" sign[22].

Kristin also put out flip-flops at her wedding. "They were honestly the biggest hit," she says. "Almost everyone took a pair, men included, for the dance floor!"

Check out Eros Wholesale or other wholesale sites for some shockingly affordable flip flops. You may have to order more than you'll need, but the unit price will still make them cheaper than ordering individual pairs from a regular clothing store.

Funny speeches are also enjoyable and memorable for guests. It's common for the Maid of Honor and Best Man to give speeches; sometimes the bride's or groom's parents will also say something (even if it's just a brief, cordial welcome). But if a particular friend or relative is funny and good at public speaking, you can ask him or her to say something at the wedding.

---

[22] I am firmly against anyone over the age of five being publicly barefoot; I also believe that you deserve the pain of your footwear choice, but again, that's something for my therapist.

You can also ban anyone who really *shouldn't* make a speech. I once attended a wedding where a dad began his speech with, "The 1400s were a difficult time," and I knew we were in for a doozy. Also, keep in mind that no guest wants to sit through an hour of speeches, regardless of who's talking. (For more about speeches, see Chapter Twenty-Two.)

You could also let more friends and family members give speeches at your rehearsal dinner. I have attended two such dinners in which the bride and groom opened up the microphone to everyone. This is more informal, involves less pressure and can result in some heartfelt moments. Just be aware that your old college roommate may really want to talk about The Naked Nacho Incident of 2004.

Now, let's talk about the HIGHLY CONTROVERSIAL wedding afterparty. I might be in the minority, but I am not a fan of these casual, post-reception gatherings. I have never been to a wedding afterparty that was as fun as its reception - although at one afterparty I did get some hot goss about the childhood friend of the groom I'd just publicly made out with in front of my entire family. Turns out he had just broken off an engagement! She was cray and more interested in weddings than marriages! As a single person writing a book about weddings, I have no idea what this might be like. I should put this in my OKCupid profile, right?

POINT IS, wedding afterparties can be hella awkward. Everyone is tired and wants to go home. They've been hanging out with you for like eight hours. What is this, Coachella[23]? Guests have to pay for drinks. The lighting is bad. Everyone's makeup has melted. And if you're at a bar that's open to the public, some drunk dude will probably hit on you and/or say weird shit about his divorce. WHAT PART OF THIS IS FUN? I hate to break it to you, but guests who attend your afterparty are doing it out of obligation and not because they actually want to go. And if a bunch of your guests don't go, are you going to be disappointed? Maybe you'll be blissfully drunk and not care what happens. I hope that's the case! But I don't want a disappointing dive bar to make your wedding end on a lame note. Also, don't you want to go bang your new spouse?

I know what you're going to say: I want an afterparty! I want to keep the fun going! I want more quality time with my best friend who lives in whereverthefuck who I never get to see! And I have literally my whole life to bang my new spouse![24]

Okay, fine. If your bridal party members/BFFs are fun, nocturnal weirdos, I can see how an afterparty could be fun. And if you're not doing

---

[23] Feel free to substitute Comic-Con for this reference

[24] I've seen bachelorette party banners that say "SAME PENIS FOREVER," which is kinda gross but also pretty hilarious.

some kind of farewell brunch, you might want to maximize your time with out-of-town-guests. "The best part of our wedding was visiting with family and friends," says the groom from New Mexico. "Some of them came a long way to attend, and it meant a lot to realize how much we all mean to each other." Also, let's be real. Going to a bar is free for you, while each additional hour of your wedding reception will cost money.

If you really want to have an afterparty, try to choose a location that is a short walking distance from your venue (or provide a shuttle). Arranging a taxi in an unfamiliar city at midnight on a Saturday can be a pain; guests will also need to figure out how to get from the afterparty location to their hotel.

If you're inviting all your guests to your afterparty, make sure you put all the info on your wedding website (and consider including the info with your invitation). If you're only inviting a select group, you can be less formal – but you might want to send a group email or text so that people know when it is and that they're invited. I've been to some weddings where the afterparty felt like a rumor and nobody really knew if they should attend.

Ultimately, as long as you provide your guests with food, drinks and clear instructions, they're gonna have a great time at your wedding. Don't worry if they don't know each other or have super different opinions about whether guns are people. They'll bond over how much they love you – or they'll just hang out with their own peeps, which is also totally fine!

Chapter Nine

BUDGETS AND GRATUITIES

Rich people, feel free to skip this chapter. Also feel free to wire money directly to my checking account so that I can hire my favorite yoga teacher to live in my apartment, teach private sessions and quote Taylor Swift to me (just kidding, he's more of a Demi Lovato guy). The rest of us need to stick to a budget. Booooooooooooooooooooooooooooo.

Your budget will vary based on location, guest count and priorities. Most brides and grooms I spoke to ended up spending more money than they originally planned, so you may want to low-ball your budget.

One thing that couples don't talk about much: how do you actually pay for the wedding? Like, how do you travel back in time and become a software engineer instead of a blogger? How do you reverse a decade of financial decisions that began with $300 worth of inflatable tiki decorations for your sophomore year dorm room?

The internet hasn't helped me with the whole time travel thing (should I watch *Looper* again and pay attention this time?). However, one Buffalo, NY bride offered a solid money-saving plan: "My fiancé and I took the amount of money the venue costs, broke it in half and then calculated how much we each needed to save bi-weekly from our paychecks in order to have that money in time for the wedding," she says, adding that she was able to save the needed money post-engagement because her wedding didn't take place until 18 months after she procured that sweet finger rock.

"We then set up direct deposits through our work to have that bi-weekly amount go directly into savings account," she says. She recommends online-only savings accounts such as Capital One or Ally, since they offer higher interest rates than accounts at traditional banks. Also, if you put your money in an account you don't have easy access to (i.e. no debit card or nearby

ATM), you won't be able to dip into your wedding savings for ramen or IPAs. I'm not saying this is easy – but I want you to have a plan.

Another bride said she opened up a new credit card specifically for the wedding that offered a 0% APR for one year. She didn't have to pay it off immediately to avoid incurring a lot of extra debt; the card also helped her keep track of exactly how much she spent. She and her mom were both authorized users, which cut down on "Can I buy this" conversations. Even with a designated card, though, you will probably want to record all wedding-related purchases in a spreadsheet.

In the past, tradition has dictated that the bride's parents should pay for the wedding. A recent survey found that parents still cover about 2/3 of the wedding budget, with parents of brides spending more (43%) than parents of grooms (23%)[25]. Lame! The couples contribute the rest.

Some couples feel guilty about accepting financial assistance. If you really feel like your parents can't afford it (you may not want them to use credit cards or retirement savings), you can try to convince them to contribute less. But keep in mind that even though you've been an Independent Woman™ since the first round of American Idol, your parents might really WANT to pay, at least for some. They want you to be happy. And maybe your parents got jobs back when they came with things like health insurance and pensions!

Just don't take parental contributions as a blank check; things could get tense if your parents agree to pay for an entire $20,000 wedding but then the budget balloons to $30,000. "Expect that everything is going to be much more expensive than you planned for, and try to save more in the beginning to have a cushion for expensive things that are sure to come up later in the process," says a bride from Los Angeles.

Alissa says that flowers were a lot more than she expected, for example. For another bride, it was shuttles.

"I was surprised at the extent to which facilities pass in obvious venue costs in the form of inflated food/drink prices (and minimal catering options)," says Rob from Minneapolis, MN. "Per-person food costs are exorbitant at the really nice places. I've had to tiptoe around intra-family disagreements about the feasibility and affordability of pricier venues."

In fact, your biggest costs will be the venue and catering, so you may want to start there. Check out Wedding Wire, The Knot, Yelp, Facebook and local vendor websites to get quotes and vendor price ranges so you can start putting together a rough budget outline.

---

[25] Lepore, Meredith. "Here's How Much Parents Pay For Their Children's Weddings." *Brides.* 5 September 2017. https://www.brides.com/story/how-much-parents-pay-for-their-childrens-weddings

"The first thing I do when I consult with brides is ask which things are most important to them," says Gina. "Then, based on that, I help them decide where to put their money."

For example, if you want a raucous dance party, she recommends choosing a Saturday night, offering liquor in addition to beer and wine, and having a band or DJ (instead of just plugging in your phone). She's seen brides end up unhappy because they said something was important but then made money-saving choices that were at odds with their priorities.

Every couple is different. If you don't care about dancing, maybe you could spend less on entertainment and more on food. But Gina says you have to think about wedding planning as if it were house hunting. "You're not going to get everything on your list," she says, adding the hardest part of wedding coordinating is dealing with unrealistic expectations. Pick your priorities and say "fuck it" to everything else so that you have enough energy to stay hydrated and fight the patriarchy.

"No one is going to remember the color of the plates, or what the centerpieces looked like, or if the invitations were pretty," says Erica. "Spend the budget on the food, drinks, and entertainment - those are the party makers!"

A bride from London, UK, agrees: "Put all the money into having a free bar for everyone."

Most couples told me that you shouldn't skimp on the photographer, either. "Pick a GREAT photographer," says Francesca. "That's the one thing we splurged on. Photos will stay forever. No one will remember your centerpieces or favors or if you had a custom-made wedding topper. Don't spend too much money on that stuff. Guests want to have a good time. Pick a great DJ/band and keep your guests entertained."

Guests also enjoy activities and extras, like photo booths, ice cream trucks, party games and fireworks shows. But these things can add up, so you may want to pick one special extra or activity as opposed to several. You can also find a budget-friendly way to incorporate a more expensive extra, like putting up a decorated selfie wall with good lighting in place of an entire photo booth. Or you could borrow a freezer and put out ice cream bars guests can grab themselves instead of hiring two people to man an artisan cart.

Don't assume that anything is included. Some caterers also provide tables, chairs and linens, but others do not; you might need to rent these items – even the buffet table the food sits on – from your venue or a separate rental company. You may also have to purchase liability insurance, depending on venue policies and local laws. If you already have renters or homeowners insurance, you can likely purchase an inexpensive policy through your provider. If not, you can look into companies like WedSafe. Note that some policies exclude liquor liability.

Consider making a few big, decisive budget-conscious decisions instead of trying to save money at every turn. Cut 25 people off your guest list, for example. One such decision will save thousands so that you won't have to agonize over a hundred different small decisions along the way. "There's no way to save money on a 200 person wedding unless you go very low key and unconventional," says Leah. "Trying to save money here and there will just result in stress and money spent to adapt to your money-saving ideas."

Or, if you want to save with every possible decision, follow Beth's advice: "Whatever is cheaper is the right choice," she says.

Be sure to budget for gratuities. "The tipping part of everything is expensive, and you're expected to tip many of the vendors," says a Los Angeles bride. "Also, many caterers include a service charge in your bill, but this usually does NOT include tip. So plan on tipping on top of the original bill." She says her catering gratuity was her biggest tip expense.

In fact, automatic catering service charges can range from 15-25% — which could equate to several thousand dollars — and these often do not include tips. Some catering contracts will include separate costs labeled "service charge," "administrative fee," or "gratuity," while others will just include a blanket "service charge." Ask your caterer explicitly if charges cover tips and if the tips are given to all staff members. You can also ask your wedding planner or coordinator to help you understand all charges. Go through everything BEFORE you pay a deposit to lock in your venue.

One of the pitfalls of choosing a venue that requires you to buy an all-inclusive package with items such as linens, stemware and cake is that you'll be required to pay a gratuity on EVERYTHING. You're not expected to tip a baker, for example, but if your venue provides a cake with your package and then charges you a 20% service charge on top of everything, you'll be paying an extra 20% for the cake, too. Read contracts carefully so that your budget can handle built-in gratuities. Put them in your Excel document! Don't accidentally tip anyone twice.

I understand why you'd want to run screaming from an all-inclusive venue, but choosing a blank space or outdoor venue that requires you to bring everything yourself may end up costing more in the long run. For example, you might have to allocate additional funds for power outlets, portable bathrooms, chair rentals, kitchen equipment, cleaning services and parking services.

"One bride told me that she wanted a dance party but then chose a campsite with nothing but dirt," Gina says. "We had to bring in a literal floor."

Below is an approximate guide for tipping vendors without contractually defined gratuities. You may also want to talk to friends who've gotten married in your specific region. I'm going to assume that you don't plan to give any unnecessary tips, so I've only listed vendors that typically DO get tips.

You are NOT expected to tip wedding planners, bakers or florists. You are also not expected to add a tip on top of any service that already includes a gratuity. That said, feel free to tip anyone you feel has done an exceptional job. You can also show your appreciation by writing social media posts about your vendors, recommending them to friends and writing positive reviews online. (You can do this for humorous wedding book authors, too!)

Note: Percentages all refer to the bill total BEFORE sales tax is added.

- Caterer – 15-20% on top of the bill total or $10-20 per employee (for people not being tipped through another fee)

- Bartender (if not part of catering) – 10-15% of the bar bill, to be split evenly

- Delivery or rental staff member who is not employed by caterer or venue (cake delivery, chair and tent setup, etc.) - $5-20 per person

- Hair or makeup artist – 15-20%

- Photographer, Videographer or Assistant who does not own the company (you don't need to tip a company owner) - $50-200

- Religious officiant - $50-500 donation to their church

- Non-religious officiant - $50-100

- Officiant who is a friend or relative - gift

- Transportation (limo, shuttle, etc.) – 15%

- Band or DJ – 10-15% or $50-150

- Individual musician or performers (if not part of an overall band tip) - $15-50 per person

- Valet attendant - $1-2 per car

- Bathroom or coat check attendant - $1-2 per guest

Gratuities that are not pre-set in contracts should be paid upon delivery, or, if the vendor is staying for the reception, at the end of the night. Designate someone to take care of final payments, which should be kept in a secure place. If a gratuity is a percentage of the total bill, such as a bar tab, you'll need to wait to see how much tequila Uncle Randy drank and mail a tip later.

If you are providing tips for bartenders, make sure to tell them not to put out tip jars for guests. Similarly, if you're tipping valets, put out a sign to let guests know they shouldn't provide additional tips.

Brides.com suggests that you also tip your catering or venue manager $250-500, provided s/he is not also serving as your wedding coordinator[26]; The Knot suggests $200-300[27]. However, this seems excessive to me if you're already tipping 15-20% on the top of your total catering bill. If you're tipping individual catering staff members instead of tipping on top of the total bill, this manager tip makes more sense. If you're not tipping on top of the total bill, Wedding Wire suggests that you tip servers/wait staff $20 or more[28]. Bridal Guide suggests $20-50 per server and $50-100 per chef[29].

Beyond gratuities, watch out for additional costs buried in contracts. Says a Los Angeles bride: "If you choose to go with a band (which I definitely recommend), just make sure you read the fine print of the contract to see if they expect certain line items that can also add up in the final budget, such as a break room or stage." She was also surprised to discover that she needed to hire a separate DJ for the time the band wasn't playing.

Talk to your partner about what you want BEFORE you meet with vendors. "I wish I knew how specific you have to be when you meet with vendors," says Lauren. She also said that her DJ was terrible. "He played music like it was a high school dance and wouldn't listen to my husband or my mom about changing it." See if yours will let you choose the playlist!

[26] Mackey, Jaimie. "The Complete List of Which Wedding Vendors to Tip – And How Much. *Brides*. 1 September 2017. https://www.brides.com/story/complete-list-wedding-vendors-gratuity-tip-how-much

[27] "Your Wedding Vendor Tip Cheat Sheet." *The Knot*. https://www.theknot.com/content/wedding-vendor-tipping-cheat-sheet

[28] Forrest, Kim. "Exactly How Much to Tip Wedding Vendors: A Complete List." *Wedding Wire*. 24 January 2017. https://www.weddingwire.com/wedding-ideas/wedding-tipping-guide

[29] Silber, Allison. "Cheat Sheet For Tipping Wedding Vendors." *Bridal Guide*. https://www.bridalguide.com/blogs/the-budget-guru/how-to-tip-wedding-vendors

Chapter Ten

AMANDA'S ULTIMATE LIST OF MONEY-SAVING TIPS

If you're not my mom, you're probably reading this book to find out creative ways to save money. Below is my ultimate list! Again, if you want to splurge on any particular thing, YOU DO YOU. Don't @ me. (Actually, please @ me on Twitter @amandapendo and also tell all your friends and frenemies about this book.)

Reduce the size of your guest list.
This is hands-down the easiest way to save money, since every per-head item (food, alcohol, invitations, favors, thank-you cards) will cost less with a smaller guest list. A lower guest count also means fewer tables and chairs, which in turn means fewer linens and centerpieces. And you'll need fewer servers and bartenders, which translates to lower vendor rates and fewer tips.

Reduce the size of your bridal party.
You'll spend less on gifts, hair and makeup, bouquets, boutonnieres and limos/shuttles.

Stay in your backyard.

Venues are expensive; if you get married in your own backyard (or a friend's), you'll save a ton[30]. You can also look into other cheap venues such as fire halls, church halls, community centers, parks, etc. See if you know anyone who's a member somewhere and has access or a special discount.

Serve a buffet or family-style meal.

"There are definitely ways to save with the catering that we chose not to do," says a bride from Los Angeles. "We chose a plated, sit-down dinner, which was more expensive than other options, but I did not expect it to be as expensive as it turned out to be."

Go homemade.

It's not a low-stress option, but you or your family could cook the food. You could also serve hors d'oeuvres instead of a full meal.

Keep it short and sweet.

Many reception venues offer a standard reception time and charge for additional hours; others might charge by the hour. Five hours is generally standard for a reception – but shorter receptions cost less. Consider cutting out speeches or designated dances, or just have less general party time later. Also, an afterparty at a local bar, as much as they annoy me, can keep the fun going for free.

Don't go crazy with flowers.

Consider mixing florals with other things. "Our centerpieces cost less than we had allotted in our budget because we did half tables with floral arrangements and half DIY centerpieces with photo collages of our friends who were seated at those tables," Francesca says.

Ask your florist for advice about how to stay in budget. Another bride says she was open to a variety of flower options, so her florist had no trouble staying in budget (choosing out-of-season flowers will cost more). If your dinner tables are rectangular, you can also opt for greenery/garlands instead of flowers, or you can reuse your bridesmaid bouquets. A florist told me that bouquets will look too small on standard round tables, though.

Alternatively, you can save money with completely non-floral centerpieces. Consider seashells, paper flowers, candles, lanterns, etc. Get creative! Also, find out if your venue can supply any décor items for free. One bride says that her venue, a restaurant, regularly has maritime lanterns

---

[30] I know that not everyone has a yard, I live in Los Angeles and have literally never had a yard, just shared rooftops I've gotten in trouble for partying on, I GET IT, OK!

on its tables. The venue coordinator let the bride borrow them for her centerpieces; she only had to supply the candles to put inside.

You could also arrange your own flowers. One crafty bride I know bought wildflowers at a big city flower market the day before her wedding and made her centerpieces and bouquet herself. She spent just over $100 and they looked great! Grocery store flowers are also an option. Some stores will arrange and deliver flowers, while others can place orders for you to pick up and DIY.

Exercise restraint with décor.

You can save money with DIY décor, but it can be an absolute time and money pit if you order everything you see on the internet, if items end up arriving broken, or if your craft projects turn out different from what they look like on Pinterest. Please only delve into the world of DIY if you legitimately ENJOY making crafts. And I know I told you to save on flowers, but I will also note that I once attended a wedding in Central New York with flowers so gorgeous that NO other décor was necessary – the tables were plain wood and the linens were plain white and it was all beautiful. Even with the fancy flowers, the bride might have actually saved money by not including any additional décor.

You might also save by choosing a venue that you think is beautiful on its own and doesn't need to be dressed up – restaurants and outdoor spaces can be great for this. You don't need to pay extra to add up-lighting if your venue already has cool lighting.

Reuse others' décor – then sell it!

Check wedding recycle websites, garage sales, thrift stores and scrap exchanges for pre-owned items like candle holders and chalkboard signs. You can also sell the décor you use to make some money back! See the appendix for info.

Collect promo codes.

Resist the urge to buy things the moment you discover them online. Join email lists and check wedding blogs to get promo codes. Wait for sales. "I spent less on DIY than I estimated by working coupons and sales," says Kristin. Another bride recommends Ebates, which gives you cash back when you shop at partner sites.

Skip the signs.

Signs like "welcome to our wedding" or "this way to love" can be adorable (and make for cute photos), but are they really necessary? Have you ever walked up to ten rows of white chairs and thought "Oh man, I have no idea where the wedding ceremony's going to be?" If you're in some rustic hobbit forest[31], signs could prevent people from getting lost, but I've seen a lot of signs at obvious banquet halls. Also, if your nuptials take place at a venue with multiple weddings happening at once, the venue will likely provide signage to direct guests.

You can also skip printed dinner menus, since it's not as though guests will be allowed to order items they didn't already RSVP for. "The paper goods ended up costing more than I had anticipated," Jen says. "This includes invitations, decorations, thank you cards, programs, menus, signage, etc." Also, thank you cards don't have to be wedding-themed or emblazoned with your face. Regular ones are cheaper!

Avoid a summer Saturday.

One wedding venue in Malibu, CA charges a full $1,000 less if you get married between November and April. And if you get married indoors, weather doesn't matter! Many venues also offer discounts on Fridays and Sundays during peak wedding season. Think about whether you want out-of-town guests to have to take off work, but for weddings of mostly local guests, creative scheduling can work well. I once attended a lovely Southern California ranch wedding on a Sunday; it was more of a mellow dinner than a raucous drunken dance party, but it seemed to fit with the couple's vibe. You can also look into Sundays before holidays such as Labor Day and Memorial Day. Or do a morning brunch wedding. Donuts and pancakes and bacon – oh my!

Ask friends and family to help.

Be careful giving important tasks to amateurs, but if you have friends who are bartenders, musicians, etc., they might be happy to donate services. You could also make a trade; one upstate New York bride used her airline points to buy a flight for one of her bridesmaids, a professional hair stylist, in exchange for styling services.

Just remember that you might not be able to be as honest with friends and family members as you can with professionals. If your aunt makes your cake, will you be able to tell her that it looks like SpongeBob Squarepants got attacked by a flower crown? Don't let a wedding spoil your relationships. Also, family members might not behave the way professionals would. "My stepdad was the DJ, and he lost the entire playlist, but instead of telling me so I could email him a new copy, he just chose songs at random," says Emily.

Be cheap in front of your parents.

---

[31] Um have you SEEN Sean Parker's wedding?
https://www.vanityfair.com/news/2013/09/photos-sean-parker-wedding

One groom told me that since he and his wife aren't big drinkers, they didn't want to spend a ton on alcohol. I'm not sure if this was calculated, but when he mentioned to his in-laws that he and his fiancée were planning to serve only soda, the in-laws were so appalled that they immediately offered to pay for an entire top-shelf bar. Win win! I'm not saying you should be a manipulative brat, but... if you told your mom, "I just can't afford a veil," maybe you'd get a free veil? OK FINE, I'M TELLING YOU TO BE A MANIPULATIVE BRAT.

Ask for vendor recommendations.

Ask your venue about their preferred vendors, who may offer you a discount. Friend referrals can also result in reduced rates.

Hire up-and-coming vendors.

If you're willing to give a student photographer or other newbie a chance, you might be able to score a deal. Carolyn says she saved on her photographer by dangling the value of a lesbian wedding in the photographer's portfolio. Similarly, a photographer might give you a discount because they want to add your venue to their portfolio.

Serve just wine and beer.

Many couples omit hard liquor from the bar at their weddings, serving just beer and wine (just remember Erin's tequila-swilling dad!). Another good idea is to serve nice champagne for the toast but cheaper champagne later. You can also offer one or two signature cocktails so you only need to buy a couple kinds of liquor rather than stock an entire bar. Other ways to save on alcohol include reducing the time of your wedding (maybe you don't need that final hour) and closing the bar during dinner. Don't do a cash bar, though. I know I've said YOU DO YOU, but that's just tacky.

Cut down on bridal party gifts.

The internet may pressure you to buy adorable "will you be my bridesmaid" gifts – hair ties, cards, champagne labels, etc. – but even as a double Maid of Honor, I can say that none of it is necessary. Go with only a card or even just have a heartfelt face-to-face, video chat or phone call! Right before the wedding, a gift such as a necklace or watch to wear on the day can be nice, but you don't need to buy everything you've seen them on Etsy and Pinterest. Matching robes make for a cute photo – and I actually still sometimes wear the one I got as MOH – but some maids might prefer you pay for their hair or makeup as a gift[32].

Recycle and borrow accessories.

Got a pair of silver heels? Wear 'em instead of buying white bridal shoes you'll never wear again! You might also wear jewelry or use a clutch you already own. You can also look into borrowing items from friends and family members.

Skip favors.

Can you even remember the favors you've gotten from weddings? Okay, I'll be honest, I do still drink from a glass that says "Gary and Kate est. 2005," and I enjoy edible favors like chocolates. But overall, guests won't care if you skip the favors – and if you have a lot of guests coming in from out of town, they won't want to put extra things in their suitcases. I love the idea of custom wine bottles, but they can't be packed in carry-ons (thanks, terrorists!). Ultimately, skipping favors is an easy way to save $100-$500.

In lieu of favors, another fun idea is to donate to a charity that means something to you and your partner (and display a card somewhere explaining this to your guests). I especially like the idea of picking a super progressive nonprofit that will make certain relatives feel uncomfortable, but that's just me.

Skip hotel welcome baskets.

Again, they're a lovely gesture – but they're not necessary. You might also consider having one basket of community items for everyone that's kept in a single bridal party suite or at the front desk, if the hotel allows.

Serve sheet cake.

The wedding cake you take photos with doesn't need to be big enough to serve all your guests. Opt for a small cake and then buy an additional undecorated sheet cake to pass out along with it. Nobody will know or care, since cake is cake! You can also save by choosing buttercream over fondant, or save by going to a grocery store instead of a fancy bakery. I served a $20 supermarket cake at my 30th birthday because I'm fancy, and everyone raved about it. I got to make a joke about "this AMAZING new

---

[32] It's generally standard to pay for bridal party hair and makeup if you REQUIRE that it be done professionally. But if maids can choose whether to use your pro or do their own, you don't have to foot the bill.

bakery...RALPH'S" and found myself very hilarious indeed.[33] You could also consider skipping a cake topper or getting a generic topper rather than a personalized one.

Also, don't forget about delivery costs. Choosing a bakery close to the venue might help – or perhaps a relative or friend could pick up the cake for you. You'd also save on a delivery driver tip!

Skip the cake completely.

Don't serve cake if you hate cake! If you still want a dessert, you might consider cupcakes, an ice cream cart or a dessert bar with multiple options. One bride says she had to have Paula's Donuts at her wedding since they're a local delicacy in Western New York. Similarly, a groom was excited to feature Salt & Straw ice cream since the company is based in his hometown of Portland, Oregon.

Cut down on other food extras.

It's tempting to offer your guests cake AND a dessert bar AND artisan ice cream AND late-night tacos AND In-And-Out Burger (or, as my dad calls it, Stop-And-Go Burger). But is any of it necessary? Pick one. Or zero.

Skip the shuttles.

It's a nice gesture to offer shuttle service when you have a lot of out-of-town guests staying at a hotel that's not walking-distance from your venue. But they're never required; just offer travel advice on your wedding website. Also, remember that shuttles will require a gratuity.

Skip engagement photos.

Yes, they're gorgeous – but since you're going to have professional photography at your wedding, you might not need official engagement photos as well. Consider sending a save the date without a photo or using a photo you already have. You could also see if a friend has a high-quality camera and can snap a few unofficial pics when you're outside in "golden hour" lighting - approximately the first hour of light after sunrise and the last hour of light before sunset. That said, one bride told me she was glad she splurged on an engagement session because it helped her camera-shy groom get some practice ahead of their wedding day.

---

[33] I also went to Catalina and back that day not knowing it would be a pukey TWENTY-NINE MILE boat ride from Long Beach, so forgive my lame joke and also feel free to use it at your wedding.

Skip the videographer.

Many people enjoy "highlight" videos for social media or permanent footage of speeches, and one bride told me that she regretted not hiring a videographer. Another bride realized that if strangers' videos were making her cry, she definitely needed one of the people she loved. However, some couples find that professional photographs and guests' cell phone videos are enough. (Maybe ask a specific friend to record the speeches instead.) You could also write a long journal entry about everything the day after your wedding so that you don't forget the details!

Get a photography package.

You might want to hire a photographer early on, especially if you are doing engagement photos, because you might be able to save on a package by using the same photographer for both the engagement session and the wedding.

Hire a photographer for fewer hours.

Some photographers may require that you hire them for a set 8 hours or a full day, but others may let you book them for 4, 5 or 6 hours. Maybe you don't care about "getting ready" photos! Just make sure to account for the time it will take your photographer to travel, set up shots, scout for good lighting, etc.

You might also want to add a few all-guest dances before dinner to capture some dancing photos early so that the photographer can leave.

Skip paper invitations.

One bride told me that getting physical response cards back was one of the most fun parts of wedding planning, but if they're not important to you, consider doing all-online invitations and RSVPs. A lot of people forget to send back response cards, anyway! You can always call or mail paper information to older relatives who might not be tech-savvy, but for younger guests, you can use Evite, Paperless Post or even a classic BCC email[34].

Skip the welcome dinner or farewell brunch.

A rehearsal dinner is standard for close family and bridal party members, but you don't necessarily need to host a dinner or farewell brunch for all out-of-town guests. These can be lovely, but prices can add up quickly. Instead, you might consider inviting everyone to a casual bar or restaurant the night before the wedding where you pay for just drinks or offer a cash bar.

---

[34] For the love of God, make sure it's BCC and not CC, or friendships will end in the reply-alls.

Remember that nothing is required.

Most brides will tell you to splurge on a makeup artist, but if you like doing your own makeup, go for it! If riding in a limo isn't important to you, take a Lyft! If you think veils are hideous, don't drop $1,000 on a veil! Uphold whatever traditions mean something to you but don't feel beholden to ones that don't. You'll save a ton of money.

Chapter Eleven

YOUR PHOTOGRAPHER

After venue and catering, your next-most important wedding planning decision is probably your choice of photographer. Years after your wedding, your photos the only thing you'll still have! Oh, and I guess you'll have a spouse. Those photos tho!

As you browse websites and portfolios, look for a photographer who captures the kind of mood you want in your wedding photos. Do you want them to be lighthearted and candid, or dramatic like a *Vogue* photo shoot?

"If want your wedding captured in a joyful, bright way, don't hire a dark and moody photographer who pulls serious expressions out of their couples," says Jenna Hidinger, a wedding photographer based in Pittsburgh, PA.[35] "Make sure you like the posing, expressions, colors, and compositions you see – because that's similar to what you'll be getting!"

Jenna says that if you're not sure what mood you want, you should try to figure out the common theme among the photos you like. (A Pinterest board could help with this.) "Make a list of common adjectives and use them as a guide while looking through wedding photographer portfolios," she says.

Look for a photographer who has experience with seasons and locations similar to yours. "If you're getting married in the winter in downtown Pittsburgh and you've only seen bright and sunny summer farm weddings from your photographer, you might want to ask to see more work that aligns with the timeframe and style of your wedding," Jenna says. "It's important to know that your photographer can handle your type of wedding, not just one

---

[35] For more advice and insight from Jenna, check out her awesome blog at http://www.jennahidingerphotography.com

style!" She recommends that you look for consistent work in a photographer's portfolio – multiple galleries or albums – with the style you're looking for.

Jenna also says that you don't need to send your photographer an enormous shot list or Pinterest board. "Pinterest is wonderful to use as inspiration – but I think it can make many brides (including myself!) try to force themselves, their weddings, and their photos into a box," says Jenna. "I work with the most amazing clients, but once, a well-meaning bride sent me a 40-page document with 'must-have' wedding photo ideas. All of the photos were taken in different styles, different lighting, and some were in locations that didn't even resemble where she would be getting married. When brides ask photographers to recreate a bunch of random photos, they run the risk of missing out on what makes their wedding unique."

She says it's more productive to use Pinterest for just a few must-have photo ideas. Remember that your photographer's job is to capture the reality and individual emotion of your wedding, not just the "perfect" moments! Your wedding should inspire your photographs, not the other way around.

Also, make sure that you enjoy your photographer's personality so that wedding-day interactions aren't awkward. "It would be awful to have someone follow you around on one of the biggest days of your life when you don't even like them," Jenna says. "You don't have to be BFFs, but actually liking your photographer will help make your day so much more enjoyable!" Jenna recommends that you look through a photographer's website/social media AND talk to them on the phone or in person so that you get a sense of the personality as well as their work.

In fact, Jenna's biggest piece of advice is that you should hire a photographer you like and trust. "Both are key," she says. "You can trust that someone will do a good job, but not like their personality – which can make you feel uncomfortable on your wedding day. Or, you can like someone's personality but not fully trust them to do a good job – and you want to make sure you have something beautiful to show for your time and money."

In the last chapter, I talked about how you might be able to hire a photographer for fewer hours to save money – but what will you miss out on? "Eight hours seems to be the perfect amount of time for photographing the essentials: getting ready, bridal details[36], the ceremony, family formals, bridal party, bride and groom portraits, and the reception," Jenna says. Traveling can also shorten this timeframe. "But most photographers have a certain amount of time they prefer for each portion of the day, and before you choose your photographer, it's important to know what those timeframes look like. Opting for less time (for example, four to six hours) instead of booking a full day coverage can mean missing out on large chunks

---

[36] Bridal details are photos of your dress, shoes, rings, invitation, etc.

of the story and what the day really looked like in full." If you're considering a photographer who offers multiple timeframes, talk to him or her about what you might have to exclude if you book less time.

Jenna also warns against hiring a photographer for less time but then expecting the same amount of work you'd get in a full day. The photos you love in a photographer's portfolio might not be from a four-hour session. "What most people don't realize is that photos take time," she says. Even photos of your dress and shoes require styling, scouting the perfect spot, rearranging, etc. Your photographer will have to repeat this process many times throughout the day.

If you or your partner is camera shy but you can't afford an engagement session for practice, Jenna suggests having a friend take some photos of you together. "The sooner you can get in front of the camera and realize it's not actually that scary, the more comfortable you're likely to feel on your wedding day," she says. She also suggests that camera-shy couples look for a photographer whose photos make it seem like the couple is having fun.

Will cell phones ruin your perfect ceremony shots? Jenna says she's seen a rise in "unplugged" ceremonies – but "a phone-free ceremony is really the couple's choice." Many couples are happy they unplugged because it let their photographers get the best shots[37].

However, one bride told me that some of her favorite ceremony photos were the ones that her friends took on their phones. Some couples were also glad they allowed guests to use phones because they weren't happy with the way their professional photos came out.

If you'd like a no-phone policy at your ceremony, you can put out a sign, put details on your website and ceremony program, and/or ask your officiant to make an announcement. Some couples worry that this sounds fussy or pretentious, but I attended a no-phone ceremony where everyone seemed happy to comply. You know your guests, though! It's also your call if you think rhyming signs about "staying present" are cute or gross. Be as cutesy or blunt as you like!

One way to compromise is to have your officiant ask guests to take photos during one designated "paparazzi" moment at the beginning of the ceremony and then request that guests put their phones away after. (They can always bring them out again when you do your recessional.)

A good photographer will likely be able to navigate around guests with phones. "I typically don't notice phones at a wedding ceremony unless someone leans out into the aisle and obstructs my shot of the bride walking

---

[37] For more about why you might want an unplugged or at least no-flash ceremony, check out this blog post (with examples of photos) from Ohio-based photographer Corey Ann: http://coreyann.com/blog/corey-talks/corey-talks-why-you-should-have-an-unplugged-wedding

down the aisle, or the groom's face when he sees his bride for the first time," Jenna says. "Yes, that has happened before – a few times with an iPad and not a phone! In those cases, if I'm close enough to the person, I'll quietly ask them not to lean as far into the aisle."

However, even if your dad isn't ruining the overall shot with his iPad, he might be preventing your photographer from capturing his candid reaction during a heartfelt moment. "I've seen parents hold phones right in front of their faces for the entirety of the ceremony, which inhibited me from getting those sweet reaction photos," Jenna says[38]. "While it's not necessarily for everyone, a phone-free ceremony gives your photographer the opportunity to get photos of your family without a phone in their face."

You might also want to privately tell your close family members to put their phones away during the reception! "I've seen many parents of the bride and groom watch toasts, first dances, and cake cutting through a phone – which always breaks my heart!" Jenna says. Of course you want guests to take photos at your kickass reception (and share them with your hashtag) – but you might want to remind your relatives that they'll be able to see professional photos of special moments. Maybe they just aren't used to this. Maybe they haven't read a million dumb thinkpieces about unplugging and now feel conflicted about it the way I do. Or maybe they're just really excited that you're not going to die alone and want to have proof!

---

[38] I honestly find this 500% more horrifying than Erin's dad bringing his own tequila to her wedding!

Chapter Twelve

HOTELS AND WELCOME BAGS

For out-of-town-guests, most couples reserve hotel blocks at one or two hotels that are convenient to the venue, making sure at least one is affordable. This ensures that your guests will be able to book rooms closer to the date of the wedding; also, if guests call the hotel and mention they're with your party, they'll get a discount. Just make sure your guests know that they can't use a third-party site like Expedia and that they might need to book over the phone instead of online. Put all travel and hotel info on your wedding website.

Some hotels allow you to reserve "courtesy blocks" of about ten rooms without paying a deposit or fee for unbooked rooms at the end. Sam from Los Angeles, CA says that one hotel didn't charge him; the only rule was that one month before the wedding, he had to let go of his claim on any unbooked rooms.

The second hotel Sam used was more complicated. If any rooms remained unbooked, he and his bride would have to pay for them (these are called "contract" or "contracted" blocks). Generally, 80% of these rooms must be reserved by a particular date or you'll have to pay for unbooked rooms.

Worried about this, Sam and his bride decided to reserve fewer rooms than they thought they would need so they wouldn't have to pay a penalty. Luckily, guests were able to figure out other accommodations. But if you want to ensure that all your guests can stay at your chosen hotels, you may end up having to pay for overestimating. Unfortunately, hotel blocks can be a surprisingly stressful part of wedding planning. Do your research to fully understand each hotel's policy. Also, be aware that some hotels won't let you book blocks more than a year in advance.

Be sure to tell your guests if there are other local events going on the same weekend as your wedding, since they may face competition for hotel rooms or other housing rentals. Also decide if you will provide a shuttle from a hotel to your wedding – this may help guests decide where to stay.

I like the idea of providing shuttles from the hotel so that guests don't have to worry about drinking too much, but wedding coordinator Gina finds them unnecessary. "Grown adults should be able to figure out their own transportation," she says, even for small towns or destination weddings. "They got from the airport to their hotel somehow." She also warns that shuttles never seem to go smoothly or stick to their schedules (another reason to hire a coordinator to deal with vendors).

Some couples like to put together hotel welcome bags or baskets for guests who travel to your wedding. "I spent A SHIT TON on welcome bags at the hotel, but it was worth it because we had a ton of out-of-town guests," says Kristin, who wanted to give each guest wine from small, local wineries but ended up choosing national wine brands to save money. She also included travel-size packs of Advil and Tums, water bottles, granola bars, and mini candy bags.

"Every guest got their own bag," she continues. "So if four friends were sharing a hotel room, they got four bags. It was basically a pregame/hangover bag but it masqueraded as a 'welcome bag.' We also planned to put flip flops in each bag but ended up just doing a giant basket of flip flops on the day."

Make sure you have a plan for distributing the bags (ask relatives or bridal party members for help), or make arrangements with the hotel front desk. Ask the hotel what it'll charge to distribute them, since this could range from $2 to $7 per bag.

Some brides have enjoyed buying personalized totes, boxes or baskets, but plain ones work fine too. Kristin notes that she once attended a wedding and forgot her custom welcome basket at the hotel by accident, so she decided to go with cheaper, non-personalized items for her own wedding.

Here are some items you can put inside hotel welcome bags or baskets:

• a welcome letter
• an itinerary for the weekend's events that includes event times, locations, dress codes, shuttle or parking information and your wedding website URL
  • promo codes for rideshare services such as Uber or Lyft
  • paper for guests to write down the hotel room info of other guests
  • information on local tourist attractions
  • maps

- snacks or candy[39]
- small bottles of alcohol
- local coffee
- spa item (candle, soap, lotion, etc.)
- sunscreen
- hand sanitizer
- bug spray
- pashmina or blanket
- fan or parasol[40]
- makeup remover or cleansing wipes
- wipe or pen for clothing stains
- travel-size pain relievers or Tums
- hangover vitamins
- bandages
- a mini sewing kit
- a bottle of water
- flip flops
- sunglasses

Keep in mind that welcome baskets are totally OPTIONAL. Plenty of guests have enjoyed out-of-town weddings sans baskets. Maybe Gina's shuttle advice can be applied to everything: grown adults should be able to figure their shit out, whether that's hangovers or acid reflux. But if assembling a bag sounds fun to you, go for it!

---

[39] Try a local favorite, the bride's and groom's favorites and/or something sold in bulk!

[40] You can also provide these at the ceremony site so guests don't have to remember to bring them along.

•

Chapter Thirteen

COLORS, THEMES, HASHTAGS AND FAVORS

I'm so glad your wedding theme is Crush the Patriarchy! We're really on the same page here.

Wedding themes are totally optional, but they can also be super fun. Most couples pick at least a color scheme, starting with bridesmaid dresses. You can then select groomsmen outfits, flowers, linens and décor pieces with this color in mind. But that doesn't mean everything has to be the same color! Orange doesn't have to throw up on your wedding.

In fact, you might want to choose a few coordinating colors. Searching "color palette" on Pinterest or "wedding color palette" on Google images will yield many gorgeous options. Am I the only person who finds calmness by browsing color palettes? Whenever your mother-in-law calls to say you "MUST" get an updo, just pull up the colors. Look at the pretty colors. Everything is fine. Colors colors colors.

You don't HAVE to pick a color scheme, either. You can absolutely pick neutral linens and just tell your florist "make it pretty." Matching invitations are also optional. You are not a prisoner of your color scheme!

Some couples also choose themes that are connected to their colors. For example, a nautical-themed wedding might feature a navy and white color scheme with accents of light blue, peach or yellow. A winter wonderland wedding might feature red, white, and silver. You could then opt for escort cards with boats, invitations with snowflakes, etc. But you could also have a theme that isn't connected to any particular color, like "spring picnic" or "France" or "I can't believe I found my husband on Tinder."

A theme could also be more of a vibe, like "rustic," "country," "backyard," "glamorous," "nightclub," "shabby chic," "industrial" or "beachy." You could also find inspiration in a favorite book, show or movie – I've seen lots of fun *Harry Potter* wedding pics! Or your theme could embody the styles of a vintage era, like the sparkle and geometry of 1920s art deco[41].

If you're stumped but still want a theme, consider developing one from a décor object or more abstract idea. Maybe you'll find a cool globe at a thrift store that evolves into a travel theme. Or maybe you could make table numbers from old book pages because you and your partner met while working at a bookstore. A theme of "love story" could then permeate your wedding. Or not! Maybe that sounds cheesy AF to you. Maybe you just want sparkles. Sparkles never go out of style!

Regardless of theme, any décor pieces can be incorporated into your wedding. Two friends of mine love their mutt, Maynard, but knew that the noise of a reception would be too much for his precious ears. They decorated a fancy ballroom foyer with cardboard cutouts of Maynard so that he'd be part of the night. Guests loved taking photos with him! It's not as though their wedding was dog-themed (but if you want a dog-themed wedding, you do you!). Another couple I know put up a cardboard cutout of THEMSELVES for additional silly photo-ops.

Themes are one of those things that some guests may not notice. If you like the idea of choosing a theme to guide your decision making, I say go for it! But please don't let a theme – or lack thereof – stress you out. If you decide on "nautical" but then decide you want non-boaty centerpieces, no one will care.

Also, don't feel like your wedding date must dictate your theme. December weddings don't require snowflakes or red, and fall weddings need not incorporate pumpkins or ghosts. My best friend got married two days before Halloween and had mostly raspberry-colored décor. It was great! You could also do a holiday theme in a different time of year, like Christmas in July – embrace the whimsy!

Below are some other ideas to inspire you.

- Carnival
- Picnic
- Garden
- Safari/explorers
- Birds or another animal

---

[41] Note that I did NOT say "Gatsby." You know the book is an INDICTMENT of excess, right? People die in the end! Did you even finish the damn thing? Call your theme "1920s" or "art deco" or "sparkly." /Rant

- Under the sea
- Nautical
- Beach/tropical
- Winter wonderland
- Fall/Halloween
- New Year's Eve
- Valentine's Day
- Mardi Gras
- Candy/sweets
- Movies/Oscars
- Broadway
- Books/stories/library
- A specific book, movie or show
- Sci-fi
- Steampunk
- Aviation, Trains or Biking
- Old Hollywood
- Art Deco
- A specific era (Victorian, 1950s, etc)
- Masquerade ball
- Tuscany
- Paris or another city you find romantic
- Your hometown
- Wine/vineyard
- Travel
- Camping
- The Old West/cowboys
- School (especially for people who met at school)
- Prom
- Astronomy/stars
- Space/aliens
- Sports
- The Olympics
- Desert
- Mountains/hiking
- Forest/trees
- Rosie the Riveter
- That chicks-only island from *Wonder Woman*
- Holly Hunter's commune in *Top of the Lake* season one
- The Spice Girls reunion
- *Runaway Bride* vs *27 Dresses*
- Can You Tell These Aren't Real Anymore
- Okay I'm done

Let's chat wedding hashtags, the absolute most important part of your nuptials! I'm always surprised at how few guests actually utilize them, but maybe we can make real, lasting change here, people. Once you pick a hashtag, put it on your wedding website, ceremony program and/or a reception sign. They're fun and let you and your guests view shared social media photos in one place. You can find a few wedding hashtag generators online, but I've found them to be pretty generic.

Try brainstorming puns related to your theme, date or wedding location. A New Year's Eve wedding might involve "countdown" or "sparkle." If you're getting married by the beach, for example, you could use "by the sea" or "shore". You could also combine your last name with a song or movie. If you're taking the last name Danner, you could use #ItsDannerTime! Some last names are admittedly easier to use than others, but a piece of your name can work, too. Lowdermilk could inspire a hashtag with the word "loud."

Wedding terms can also be helpful: think about what you can do with "hitched," "knot," "vows," "I do," "party of two," "bride," "groom," "wed," etc. Rhyming always helps! If you're taking the last name Mott, you might like #MottsTieTheKnot. If you're marrying a Nate, you can rhyme it with "fate."

Ask a friend for help – this is a fun Maid of Honor duty! It doesn't cost anything, and your MOH can help from the comfort of her couch. Just take her suggestions with a grain of salt if she's in the midst of binging *The Handmaid's Tale*. #WeirdHeadspace #UnderHisIDo

A theme might also inform your wedding favors. If your theme is movies, for example, you might give out bags of popcorn. Again, favors are optional – but you can attach favors to escort cards, give guests a small treat at their seat, or set up a table of favors near the exit. You can also get favors customized! Below are some ideas:

- Wine or beer glasses
- Shot glasses
- Mugs
- Wine bottles
- Drink koozies
- Bottle openers
- Bottle stoppers
- A bar item and the recipe for your signature cocktail
- Coasters
- Candy or other food treats
- Local condiments (like BBQ sauce, maple syrup or olive oil)
- Coffee, tea or hot cocoa
- Food kits (like for s'mores)

- Candles
- Key chains
- Photo frames
- Playing cards
- Beach towels
- Blankets
- T-shirts
- Hats
- Sunglasses
- Soap
- Lip balm
- Match boxes
- Magnets
- Playlist CDs
- Luggage tags
- Holiday ornaments
- Snow globes
- Cookie cutters
- Water bottles
- Lottery tickets
- Notebooks or journals
- Pens
- Puzzles or coloring books
- Birdseed
- Plant or seeds
- Bubbles
- Confetti poppers
- Sparklers
- Whatever you'd like to get if you were a guest!

Chapter Fourteen

YOUR WEDDING DAY TIMELINE

In this chapter, you'll find four sample wedding day timelines that you can customize as needed.

Keep in mind that if you have a wedding planner or coordinator, you won't need to create a timeline yourself – you'll likely just need to schedule hair and makeup artists and tell your bridal party members, family members and vendors when to arrive.

Allow 60 minutes for a bride's hair, 30 minutes per person for others' hair, 45-60 minutes for a bride's makeup and 30 minutes per person for others' makeup. If you've got a large group getting hair and makeup done, consider hiring a second or assistant hair and makeup artist so that these services can be done simultaneously. If you're not getting ready at your ceremony venue, allow for transportation time. Also, figure that vendors will arrive and décor will get set up while you get ready.

Don't forget to schedule a time for lunch. Ask a bridal party member, relative or wedding coordinator to bring food or order delivery. Have this person procure fun snacks, too (when I was MOH, this obviously included mimosas).

When scheduling your photographer and videographer, decide if you want "getting ready photos" (the Maid of Honor helping the bride get into her dress, a mom helping with jewelry, etc.). Also decide if you'd like photos of bridesmaids in robes or if you'd like the maids to be in their dresses when they're in the background of your these photos. For the reception, if you'd like photos of particular dances or events such as the cake cutting, make sure you've booked your photographer and videographer for enough time. You can also move these events earlier.

Most timelines agree that you'll need between one and a half and two hours for all your formal, posed photos (including a first look). This does not include transportation to or from photo areas. Also, plan for your reception to last about six hours: one hour for cocktails, two hours for dinner and three hours for dancing. The rest is up to you! Do your first dance after you eat cake if you want. Do your first dance WHILE you eat cake. Hell, do your first dance while JUMPING OUT of a cake. Just cut the cake at least two hours before your reception's end so that servers have enough time to put out slices for guests.

If you don't get to do a ceremony run-through at your rehearsal dinner (which can be hard if your rehearsal dinner is at a small location), you can fit one in after photos and before the ceremony.

Play some entrance music as guests arrive for the ceremony (about 30 minutes before the time listed on your invitation). Also make sure to tell your officiant about any announcements you'd like the guests to hear, such as telling family members to report to a particular place for photos. For the reception, make sure the DJ or band leader knows about all announcements and proper pronunciations.

During cocktail hour, you and your partner can sneak away to a private area to have a moment alone. You might also use this time to take more photos, especially if your ceremony ends just before sunset. Google the time of the sunset on your wedding day – it's something you can find out right now!

Sample Timeline 1:
-Non-Religious (Shorter) Ceremony
-Ceremony and Reception at Same Location
-Ceremony Run-Through Right before Ceremony
-Photos before Ceremony

1:45 pm	Getting Ready Photos
2:15 pm	Bridal Party Photos and First Look
4:15 pm	Ceremony Run-Through
4:30 pm	Family Photos
5:00 pm	Start Time Listed on Invitation
5:15 pm	Ceremony
5:45 pm	Cocktail Hour
6:45 pm	Move Guests to Dinner Space
7:05 pm	Introductions/Entrance and First Dance
7:15 pm	Parent Welcome Toasts
7:30 pm	Dinner and Bridal Party Toasts
8:30 pm	Parent Dances
9:00 pm	Cake Cutting, Bouquet Toss, Garter Toss or Any Other Features
9:30 pm	Dancing the Night Away!

Sample Timeline 2:
-Religious (Longer) Ceremony
-Ceremony and Reception in Different Locations
-No First Look
-Photos between Ceremony and Reception
-Receiving Line

11:45 am	Getting Ready Photos
12:00 pm	Start Time Listed on Invitation
12:15 pm	Ceremony
1:15 pm	Bride/Groom, Bridal Party and Family Photos
3:30 pm	Everyone Travels to Reception
4:00 pm	Cocktail Hour
5:00 pm	Receiving Line
5:30 pm	Introductions/Entrance and First Dance
5:45 pm	Parent Welcome Toasts
6:00 pm	Dinner and Bridal Party Toasts
7:00 pm	Parent Dances
7:30 pm	Cake Cutting, Bouquet Toss, Garter Toss or Any Other Features
8:00 pm	Dancing the Night Away!

Sample Timeline 3
-Religious (Longer) Ceremony
-Ceremony and Reception at Different Locations
-All Family Photos Done after Ceremony
-First Look

2:00 pm	Getting Ready Photos
2:15 pm	Bridal Party Photos and First Look
3:15 pm	Start Time Listed on Invitation
3:30 pm	Ceremony
4:30 pm	Family Photos (While Guests Travel to Cocktail Hour)
4:45 pm	Cocktail Hour
5:00 pm	Family, Bride & Groom Travel to Reception
5:45 pm	Move Guests to Dinner Space
6:00 pm	Introductions/Entrance and First Dance
6:15 pm	Parent Welcome Toasts
6:30 pm	Dinner and Bridal Party Toasts
7:30 pm	Parent Dances
8:30 pm	Cake Cutting, Bouquet Toss, Garter Toss or Any Other Features
9:00 pm	Dancing the Night Away!

Sample Timeline 4
-Non-Religious (Shorter) Ceremony
-Ceremony and Reception at Same Location
-Utilizes Photographer for Shortest Time Possible (About 4 hours)
-No First Look
-No Parent Speeches or Dances
-First Dance after Dinner

4:15 pm	**Start Time Listed on Invitation**
4:30 pm	**Ceremony**
5:00 pm	**Bride/Groom, Bridal Party and Family Photos (While Guests are At Cocktail Hour)**
6:15 pm	**Move Guests to Dinner Space**
6:30 pm	**Introductions/Entrance**
6:35 pm	**Dinner and Bridal Party Toasts**
7:35 pm	**First Dance**
7:40 pm	**Open Dance Floor to Everyone**
7:50 pm	**Cake Cutting (or Photos with Cupcakes)**
8:00 pm	**Dancing the Night Away!**

Chapter Fifteen

ELOPEMENTS AND NONTRADITIONAL WEDDINGS

If the idea of planning, attending or paying for an elaborate wedding makes you want to embrace the sweet release of death, good news: you have other options!

"Consider eloping or having a small wedding," says Carolyn, who had a traditional wedding for her first marriage and an elopement the second time around. "It is far more intimate and feels more special. You remember every moment because you get to focus on each other instead of trying to make sure you speak to a hundred guests."

"For my second wedding, I chose a place that treated elopements like a real wedding," she continues. "Luckily, they had all the vendors picked, and you just had to say what you wanted in terms of flowers, cake, etc. All of that was fun because we were planning just for two people instead of trying to please everyone else. For the elopement, a lot of options were $500-$1,000 for very standard packages that sort of felt like a rip-off (even though they were way cheaper than a traditional wedding). Instead, we paid $3,300 for an elopement package that was a 3-night all-inclusive package, very private, very customized, and it felt like we got WAY more than our money's worth."

Erin, who was disappointed with her wedding, agrees. "I wish I'd known that control freaks are always going to be miserable on their wedding days," she says. "ELOPE! Don't have bridesmaids! ELOPE! For the love of all that is holy ELOPE and buy out a restaurant for a night instead or not - go on a fabulous honeymoon! Ignore everyone (especially parents/nosy busybodies)."

Adds Francesca: "Wedding planning sucks. If my husband-to-be hadn't been so hands-on, I would have eloped in a heartbeat."

I am not writing this to make you stressed out about wedding planning. If eloping isn't for you, I totally get it. But if you ARE considering an elopement, I have heard only good things about the idea.

First off, you'll spend less money, meaning you'll have more to spend on a house down-payment, a honeymoon or a fully-functional Skee Ball Machine. You also won't have to SAVE as much money, meaning you can get married NOW and/or avoid incurring debt for your wedding.

You will also save yourself a lot of time and stress when it comes to managing difficult family members. If your family members, divorced parents or step-family members don't get along, you won't have to deal with warring personalities and impossible seating charts. "My uncle got angry at his mother and stormed off [during the wedding]," says Emily. Yikes!

A bride from New Orleans, LA also had some family drama at her wedding. "The relatives on one particular branch of my family didn't come to my wedding," she says. "Instead, they waited at reception hall for everyone to arrive. I walked up the aisle with my dad whispering to him how sorry I was that some of his family were no-shows."

Deirdre from Saskatoon, Saskatchewan might win the prize for most family drama: "My father-in-law tried to talk my husband out of [marrying me] and called me a bitch on the wedding day," she says. "The hall informed us no bartender would be supplied morning of, the DJ was drunk and played the same songs over and over, and a friend of my husband insisted on hanging out in our room after the wedding to watch a horror movie and would not leave us alone on our wedding night." If that's not an argument for eloping, I don't know what is. (On the flip side, your wedding probably won't be as disastrous as hers!)

One groom told me that his in-laws decided to get divorced two months before his wedding, and one relative even predicted that there'd be a beat-down at the reception. Luckily, the wedding was a success - sans fisticuffs - but the groom and his bride were stressed out throughout the entire planning process. When they renewed their vows on the beach ten years later, they invited just a handful of people and felt much more at ease.

Eloping also means you also won't have to spend a year (or more) of your life planning a big event when you have other things to do, like become the next carpet king of Wisconsin or browse eBay for a fully-functional Skee Ball machine.

"I thought planning a wedding was like buying a Lexus; you just go in and pick one out," said one father-of-the-groom during his rehearsal dinner speech. "Turns out it's like BUILDING a Lexus." Super relatable car choice, I know, but I appreciate his analogy.

Eloping doesn't mean you'll be limited to tacky or disappointing options. From Napa vineyards to Adirondack cabins, a growing assortment of elopement packages offer the wedding of your dreams. You could also be like Kristen Bell and Dax Shepard, who got hitched at the Beverly Hills courthouse for $142.[42] Just sayin!

The obvious downside of eloping is that your friends and family won't be there to celebrate with you. But maybe for you, that's a plus.

You could also consider a small affair that's somewhere between a traditional wedding and an elopement. For her second marriage, one bride tied the knot alongside just her fiancé, her daughter, her step-daughter, a photographer and an officiant. The ladies all purchased hair, makeup and nail services at an upscale hotel in Huntington Beach, CA. They got ready in the hotel's swanky spa – entry was included with their services – and then went down to the public beach for the ceremony. Afterward, they returned to the hotel and had dinner at its restaurant with just a regular reservation. They had to arrange things without the help of hotel staff, but the wedding felt like a special experience and cost considerably less than any of the hotel's wedding packages. Genius! If you aren't near a beach, you could do the same thing in a public park.

Just be aware that vendors might have more experience with traditional, large weddings. "I had a nontraditional wedding: 30 people in my living room and then a party bus to a restaurant," says Beth. "The thing I struggled with was that since I wasn't doing [something] traditional, it was very confusing for people. Ladies at stores were downright rude and offended I wasn't doing a 150-person banquet. I didn't expect that. Many things just weren't able to be scaled for the size I was looking for."

---

[42] Are Kristen and Dax the only celeb #GOALS marriage we have left?! OMG they'd better keep that shit working.

Chapter Sixteen

INVITATIONS AND STATIONERY

Invitations should be sent out 8-12 weeks before your wedding. However, you may want to arrange everything earlier to get a package discount (with both save the dates and invitations) or to make everything match. That said, it's fine if you send out save the dates before you choose your invitation design; some people are just super into coordinated stationery[43]. Be patient and wait for promo codes! All invitation sites I shopped offered them at some point.

Include reply cards or postcards with meal choices on your invitation. It is customary for you to include the return postage (postcards will be a tad cheaper). You may also want to include a card with information about rehearsal/welcome dinners, farewell brunches, hotels and transportation.

If you're not a design-oriented person, choose an invitation package that sticks to a firm template and includes envelope addressing. But if you want to get more creative and/or save some money, you can work with simpler, more customizable options from sites like Vistaprint. You could also choose to hand-address your envelopes or print out labels with your own printer. Another option is to hire a digital calligrapher – you might be surprised by how affordable this service can be.

"Our wedding had a lot of out-of-town guests, so we planned auxiliary events like a welcome party and a farewell breakfast and wanted to include detailed hotel block and transportation information – meaning extra stationery pieces," says a bride from Buffalo, NY. "When I priced it out on the traditional invitation sites, the cost was way out of my budget. I ended up going with a template on Vistaprint and then ordered customization through their graphic design service (only $5!). I was able to get a two-sided invitation

---

[43] TOTALLY unnecessary, but man, I love that shit.

with envelope, a postcard for the rehearsal dinner, a postcard for the auxiliary events, an RSVP card with envelope and a business card with our registry information, wedding URL and social media hashtag. For 225 guests, I was able to get everything for $249 because I placed my order during Vistaprint's semi-annual sale and got 40% off EVERYTHING. I felt like I hacked the wedding stationery industry. Most importantly, everything came out great, and it really matched the vibe my fiancé and I were going for."

"I wanted my envelopes to look whimsical and chic, but hand-drawn calligraphy was out of my budget," she continues. "I found a digital calligrapher on Etsy who charged about $0.40 per envelope. She provided me with a PDF sized to my invitation envelope's specifications. She included a detailed tutorial for self-printing, but my janky home printer was NOT having it. So I took that PDF file to a locally-owned print shop and they printed all my envelopes for me - both invitations and RSVP reply cards. They came out perfectly and look so professional and well-done. All in, it cost less than $100 for me to have 300 total envelopes (invitation & RSVP reply card) designed digitally and printed professionally."

Look at a few wedding invitation options or templates to get a sense of your options for wording. You can go formal or casual; you can also choose whether or not to mention middle names, parents' names or families in general:

Kindly join us for the marriage of Katie and Kenny

Together with their parents, Jessica and Amy invite you to celebrate their wedding

Together with their families, Morgan and Cory invite you to celebrate their marriage

You are cordially invited to celebrate the wedding of Tom and Matteo

Mr. and Mrs. Brad and Aisha Washington request your company at the marriage ceremony of Heather Elizabeth and Kenneth James

Curtis and Janet Smith and Dan and Alicia Jones request the pleasure of your company at the marriage of their children Amy Smith and Chase Jones

Please join us for the wedding celebration of Maria and Eric

Your presence is requested at the wedding of Becky and Susan

Alexa and José invite you to share their wedding ceremony

Ishira & Hunter
Join in our celebration of love and marriage

COME GET LIT AS IVY AND RANDALL GET HITCHED,
BITCHES!

Below this, include when and where the festivities will commence. Most planners and coordinators recommend that you list your ceremony as starting fifteen minutes before you the actual start time in your wedding timeline, just in case guests are tardy. Also mention if your reception is adults-only. It's standard to write "dinner and dancing to follow," but you can get creative here, too. I've seen one invitation that said "bites, booze and bad dance moves to follow." Alliteration AND rhyming, does it get any better? Another cute invitation for an outdoor wedding read "dinner, dancing and starlight to follow."

You can also choose a casual or formal style for how you address your envelopes:

Krista and John Smith
Mr. and Mrs. John Smith
Mr. John and Mrs. Krista Smith
Mr. John Smith and Mrs. Krista Smith

If someone's a Doctor, include that too:

Mr. Derek and Dr. Megan Badass
Dr. Megan Badass and Mr. Derek Badass

Finally, if you are letting a guest bring a plus one, you should include that on the envelope:

Ms. Sarah Singletinder and Guest
Sarah Singletinder and Guest

Be sure to leave time for approving your proof, shipping and addressing. The invitation site Minted, for example, will send you a proof within 48 hours and then begin production after you approve it. Production then takes 2-4 business days, and shipping takes 5-9 business days.

You can save a lot of money and paper with electronic-only invitations through Paperless Post or Evite. Older guests who aren't tech-savvy may need a physical invitation or phone call, but there is no reason, outside of tradition, why you HAVE to send paper invitations. When a friend of mine sent out only electronic invitations for her wedding last year, everybody figured out when and where to go. Paper invitations can be beautiful and serve as keepsakes – but if you skip them, the world will keep turning. Hell, Amy Schumer invited guests to her wedding via text message and even J-Law made it work![44] You might also be amused when your mother RSVPs online 47 times because she's so damn excited.

Whether or not you send paper invitations, guests can also RSVP online through sites like The Knot, Minted, anRSVP and RSVPify.

Don't freak out if tons of guests say yes right away. "We got a lot of RSVPs early on and were worried we were going to go over our target," says Sam. "And everyone told us not to worry, because the YESes always come early and the NOs always come late. And people cancel. But we freaked out anyway and were convinced that nobody understood. And then it turned out they were right. And then it happened to all of our friends who had weddings after us. And they freaked out, and we told them not to panic, and they panicked, and it was fine. In conclusion, you'll probably panic no matter what I say, but you shouldn't."

Be aware that some people will RSVP yes and then just not show up on the day of your wedding. Flights get cancelled, kids get sick…and some people are dicks. "The thing that surprised me the most was how many people did not show the day of the wedding," Erica says. "That seemed crazy to me!"

---

[44] Grossbart, Sarah. "Insider Amy Schumer's 'Very Laid-Back' Wedding to Chris Fischer." *Us Weekly*. 22 February 2018. https://www.usmagazine.com/celebrity-news/news/inside-amy-schumers-very-laid-back-wedding-to-chris-fischer/

Chapter Seventeen

YOUR BRIDAL PARTY

One of the best parts of getting married is celebrating with your best friends and closest family members. But who gets to be a bridesmaid or groomsman? The best way to decide is to put your friends through a physically demanding competition a la *Survivor* mixed with the sparkly evening wear of Miss United States.[45]

Or you could call your favorite people and ask them!

In the past, couples have felt obligated to choose an equal number of men and women to balance out photos – but this isn't a requirement. Your photographer will know how to make a group of two ladies and four dudes look just fine. Also, you don't have to be strict about gender rules. My best friend made her brother "Man of Honor" and had him stand with her bridesmaids. He even held her bouquet during the ceremony – and was thrilled to do so – because fuck traditional gender roles!

More important than sticking to tradition is picking the right people – and the right-sized group. You don't necessarily have to ask people to be in your bridal party just because you were in theirs, especially if it was years ago when you were closer. Many couples only choose a Maid of Honor and a Best Man or opt for family-only bridal parties. Sean says he was happy he only included siblings because it "reduced planning and eliminated the idea that some friend might get jealous."

Emily was also content with her small bridal party. "I had one bridesmaid and one groomsman, and I was happy with that," she says.

You could also skip the bridal party completely! YOU DO YOU. Just keep in mind that no bridal party might mean that you'll have to plan your

---

[45] Come on, I know I'm not the only one who watches *Miss Congeniality* every time it's on cable.

own bachelor or bachelorette party since the Best Man and Maid of Honor typically plan such shindigs. Alternatively, if you choose bridesmaids but no Maid of Honor, your maids will only be able to come to you as a point person or leader, and some brides and maids find this stressful. You might also miss out on speeches. These things are not insurmountable - just some things to consider.

No bridal party might also mean that you'll be alone (or maybe just with close relatives) when you get all dolled up on your wedding day. When my best friend got married, we had a lot of downtime in the bridal suite, so I'm glad we had a big group. "Woman" by Ke$ha came up on Spotify multiple times, making it a little awkward when the "motherfucker" lyrics came on and moms were around. Ah well, what can you do?

The answer: Drink more mimosas and text dumb photos to the philosophy professor you recently met via OKCupid. Don't worry, I didn't START with dumb drunk photos. I first asked his opinion about sweatshops because A) I feel bad about foreign-made clothes but B) I read an article about how boycotts won't help the women in Bangladesh who need those jobs. I'm full of fun, sexy topics like this! He tried to respond with an academic journal article but discovered that OKCupid's messaging system bans attachments, probably to guard against dick pics.

Managing a large group of bridesmaids also means managing their personalities. "One of my bridesmaids got a little pissy here and there at other people because she thought they were not making my wedding as good as it should be," says Jen. "So it came from a good place, but there was no reason to be abrupt."

"My bridesmaids didn't like each other," says Erin, who recommends skipping bridesmaids completely.

Also, the larger your group of bridesmaids, the harder it will be to find a bridesmaid dress that works on all body types (see Chapter Nineteen).

Serving as a bridesmaid or groomsman can cost a lot, from the dress to the bachelorette party to transportation to the wedding. Your friends might feel obligated to say yes to joining your wedding party but then complain or ask for special treatment when you ask them to buy dresses, rent tuxes, etc. Sometimes brides are unreasonable, while sometimes it's bridesmaids who are unreasonable. Please be cognizant of costs – and also remember that you can cut down on drama and stress by simply asking fewer people to be in your bridal party. This way, you'll encounter fewer surprise pregnancies, group emails, scheduling issues and weird requests. One bridesmaid asked a bride if she could change out of the dress right after the ceremony, for example. Maybe that's not something you'd care about, but it bothered the bride I spoke with.

In fact, many couples told me they had issues with their bridal party members. "Three months before my wedding, one of my bridesmaids decided she couldn't come," says the Amherst bride.

Jessica can top that: "I had to kick my Maid of Honor out of the bridal party because she could not (or would not, I'm not entirely sure) help with any of the planning or even buy her dress because she 'couldn't afford it' (even though she'd take her kids to the movies and WrestleMania often)," she says. "She then texted me two hours before the wedding to tell me that she would not be there. Really? Needless to say, we don't talk anymore. The rest of the day went perfectly!"

If you're an easygoing person, you might be amused by things that go wrong within your bridal party. "A bridesmaid almost broke her ankle night before and had to wear a walking boot," says the bride from New Orleans. "I laughed and wasn't mad (she thought I'd freak out)."

A NOTE ABOUT THE WORD "BRIDEZILLA": I mostly think it's a sexist term. If you simply expect a vendor to give you what you've paid for, how does this make you a city-crushing monster?! Would we say this about a man who expects good service? God forbid a woman isn't sweet and polite when someone drops her $500 cake in a parking lot. HOWEVER, if you forget that your best friends and family members also have their own lives and can't drop everything to decoupage table numbers, then maybe you ARE being a 'zilla. Check yourself. This goes for dudes, too!

Don't assume that people won't want to be in your bridal party just because they've been in a lot of weddings, they're significantly older or younger than you, they're pregnant or they're busy parenting a few little tyrants. One bridesmaid I know loved attending an out-of-state bachelorette party and wedding by herself because it meant she was able to sleep in a comfy bed without any husbands, kids or dogs!

To keep your bridal party members happy, stay on top of scheduling and be clear with your requests. Be respectful of budgets and try to give honest, up-front estimates of what things will cost. And if someone declines to join your bridal party because of cost, time or another reason, be gracious and accept the decision – this is better than the person begrudgingly accepting and then flaking out on important events or complaining for a year.

Remember that your bridal party members are not free DIY assistants. "I'm not a fan of putting your bridesmaids to work," says Gina. If people offer to help, that's one thing – but be mindful of everyone's schedules and interests. It might be easier to leave things to professionals.

Unless you love unwieldy email chains, don't ask the members of your bridal party for too many opinions. Sending an email to eight people asking "what do you guys want for a bridesmaid dress?" might to turn your inbox into a *Real Housewives* reunion special. It's fine to ask for some feedback, but if you're too indecisive or open-ended with questions, you may get frustrated when people don't respond or overwhelmed by all the responses. Or maybe you love reading personal emails when you're supposed to be working! Maybe Crazy Dana is microwaving salmon burgers in the kitchen again and you need to hide. YOU DO YOU!

If you'd like your bridal party members to wear specific accessories on your wedding day, it's a nice gesture to give these items as gifts. You might also consider the following:

- jewelry
- robes
- tote bags
- clutches
- makeup bags
- compacts
- cosmetics
- skincare items
- fragrances
- getting-ready kits
- hangover kits
- wine glasses
- pint glasses
- champagne flutes
- mugs
- bottle openers
- bottles of alcohol
- tea or coffee
- water bottles
- pashminas
- pocket squares
- phone cases
- candles
- socks
- slippers
- flip-flops or sandals
- flasks
- watches
- cufflinks
- sunglasses
- luggage tags
- gift cards

Most of these can be personalized. See the appendix for store and website suggestions.

Chapter Eighteen

YOUR DRESS

I have long been obsessed with TLC's *Say Yes To the Dress*. And *Say Yes to the Dress Atlanta*. And *Say Yes to the Dress UK*. And even *Keasha's Perfect Dress*, a one-season show starring a former Kleinfeld *Say Yes* consultant who defected to Toronto. Perhaps I love these shows because they let me fulfill my perpetual desire to Buy Clothes For The Life I Don't Have without actually spending money. So when my best friend began looking for a wedding gown, I was excited to use my *Say Yes*-honed expertise to help her find the perfect one. Several ladies told me that picking out a dress was one of their favorite parts of wedding planning. "It was a blast!" Erica says.

Jessica agrees: "It was so fun to get treated like a princess and wear dozens of gorgeous dresses!"

Even better news is that you don't have to spend an entire Scrooge McDuck pool of gold coins on a dress. "My dress was a lot less expensive than I was planning to pay," Jessica says.

Adds the bride from New Orleans: "Compromise on the dress. Seriously, unless you have money, you will be able to find a dress you are happy with that's very affordable. I was lucky and found mine on clearance for $300."

The original New York *Say Yes to the Dress* makes it seem like if your budget is anything less than $3,000, you'll walk down the aisle in flaming trash designed by some dude who got kicked off *Project Runway* in the pre-series casting special (get to the point, *Project Runway*, you're clogging my DVR). But this is totes untrue. Yes, you certainly CAN spend half a year's income on a diamond-encrusted frock from H.R.H. Pnina Tornai, but even fancy bridal salons have affordable options. According to The Knot, brides spent an average of $1,509 on their dresses in 2017. And if you want to spend a LOT less – maybe even as low as $150 or $200 - I have plenty of ideas for you!

Bridal salons will let you try on sample gowns; you won't actually take the dress you try on home (unless you buy the sample – more on that later). Instead, you'll place an order for a made-to-order dress that will arrive at the store in a few months. Give yourself at least a few weeks for shopping; order your dress about eight months before your wedding to leave enough time for dress production and alterations. If you wait longer, you will still have some options, such as buying a sample, buying a preowned dress or placing a rush-order for an additional fee – but many brides like to get dress shopping out of the way early.

Unless you're super rich, you'll need an approximate budget – and don't forget about alterations. "When I bought my dress (on sale), I didn't take alterations into consideration, and those are important," Carolyn says. You should also allocate money in your general wedding budget for a veil, headpiece, shoes, jewelry and undergarments.

"It really shocked me how much it cost for a veil," adds Erica. "I ended up having a really simple one made for the cheapest price possible because it seemed really silly to pay so much money for something that you wear for five minutes!"

Make sure your bridal consultant knows your budget and how tightly you want to stick to the budget. Some bridal consultants won't show you anything too expensive, but others will treat the budget like it's a ballpark figure. If you're afraid of falling in love with a dress that's too expensive, don't try on anything above your budget. You might be able to haggle with store owners for a percentage off the dress, discounted accessories or a discounted alterations package, but keep in mind that when a consultant says a dress is $1,250, this doesn't include tax or alterations.

HOWEVER, if you're not worried about making an impulsive purchase, be more flexible with what you try on. You might discover a style you love that you can find in a cheaper version in another brand, or you might find a specific dress that you can later buy preowned or as a sample. My friend tried and loved an $8,000 gown but knew she couldn't spend that much. She showed a photo of it to a consultant at another store, who picked out a similarly-shaped dress in another brand and my friend ended up buying it – for $1,400! If she hadn't tried on the expensive dress, she never would have found her ultimate fave – but she also wasn't ever gonna put 8k on her Amex, so it wasn't dangerous for her to try on the expensive gown. (Be honest.)

Designers and stores usually don't post dress prices on their websites (annoying!), but some will post price ranges, so you might be able to eliminate entire designers or stores this way. Also, with a little Internet searching, you can figure out approximate dress costs by looking at what resellers initially paid. You can also see what specific dresses look like on non-models by looking at resale sites and checking Instagram for a hashtag with the designer and dress name or style number.

Do some online research to figure out what styles you like – but honestly, too much research might be a waste. You might think you want a ball gown but then go to a store, put on two ball gowns and realize you hate them, thus rendering 400 Pinterest pins of ball gowns useless.[46] Many brides end up with totally different styles than they'd expected; one of my friends was sure she wanted lace and ended up picking a fully beaded gown with zero lace! Another bride thought she'd hate ball gowns because she's petite but discovered she loved the drama of their full skirts. Let go of the idea that any particular style is off-limits because of your shape or size. If you hate strapless gowns, that's fine – but do not feel like you have to adhere to dumb rules like "petite brides shouldn't wear ball gowns" or "busty brides shouldn't go strapless" or "you can't bring champagne to David's Bridal."

Be open-minded! Remember my friend with the $1,400 dress? She was SURE she'd buy a strapless dress, but the dress she ended up buying had thin, beaded straps – a style she never even looked at online. Who knew? FYI, straps allow a dress to have a lower back, so if you want to show off the 700 planks you've done in yoga, consider straps.

Another reason to be open-minded is that the dresses' fabrics, details and colors might look different in person than they do online. One bride I spoke to loved several dresses from a particular designer but found that they all just weren't structured enough for her curvy body, so she had to look into other brands. That said, don't let a friend or consultant talk you into something you know you don't want. I know it can be hard to stand up to a pushy mother-in-law when you're in the middle of a busy store and your back fat is falling out of a sample dress that's half your size, but stay strong. Your MIL probably wore hideous puffy sleeves at her wedding, so what does she know?!

Be picky about who you bring to your bridal appointment. Despite what reality shows tell you, you don't need an entourage of seven sassy characters. Eight is preferable. JK! One bride I know brought several relatives shopping with her, and while they were all positive and polite (ew), they each liked a different dress. It made her very confused!

Don't invite anyone who's going to insult your body, criticize your taste or just not want to be there. Your mom might want to come, but there's no standard for anyone you HAVE to include. It's a good idea to bring one friend so that s/he can take photos of you and help you remember what you tried on, but you can also absolutely try on dresses alone – for your own sanity and so that your friends or relatives don't get so tired of dress shopping that they put arsenic in your Prosecco.

---

[46] I fully admit that I probably won't take my own advice here because DRESSES. Pin away, lovelies. Just don't say I didn't warn you.

"Dress shopping is overwhelming at first, so it's okay to shop alone before bringing people into the mix," says Takla from Astoria, NY. "Trying on dresses for the first time, I was anxious and scared about how I would look - I assumed samples were all runway sizes and that what I dreamed of wouldn't work for me. But I was able to try on different styles and I felt so much better. I got more excited to bring in my mom and others for my next appointment because I had more of an idea of what I would look like. My insecurities and inhibitions were lifted."

Takla also warns brides not to get caught up in other people's feelings while dress shopping. "You should be honest right off the bat about what you like or don't like in a dress, and if you aren't feeling it, take it off ASAP," she says. "The people you bring with you are special and important, and they might get emotional seeing you as a bride for the first time. But you have to reflect on how you actually feel about the dress instead of trying to match others' reactions." She also says you shouldn't waste time letting someone put a veil on you if people like a dress that you don't.

"You should also consider how your spouse will see you as you walk down the aisle," she continues. "A wedding is about the two of you becoming one."

If you want a dress that isn't ivory, white or blush/champagne, you might want to look at special occasion dresses instead of traditional bridal gowns. If friends or relatives give you shit about your color preference, kindly inform them that brides have only been wearing white since Queen Victoria made it cool in 1840. Before then, most brides wore the nicest dress they already owned, and royals wore embroidered metallic gowns.[47]

When you shop, bring a bra and shoes that are the height you want to be at your wedding. Many brides have bra cups sewn into their dresses so they don't have to deal with weird backless bras, but you'll want to see what the front of the dress looks like when the girls are supported.

Also bring shapewear (if you plan to wear shapewear). Feminist me thinks it's kinda bullshit that one of the most successful female CEOs made her fortune by getting women BACK into girdles...but dress-loving me wants to wear slinky shapes without sucking in my stomach, and lazy me wants to keep eating gelato for breakfast. Says Kate Beckinsale, who starred in the Jane Austen movie *Love & Friendship*: "Having worn a corset the whole movie, it's so great that we don't have to wear corsets – but I feel like we now have to BE the corset, which sucks. You have to do hot yoga or whatever it is to make you the actual corset. Like, it's still oppressive." FUCK, Kate, you're so right. You're also getting pretty deep for a Stephen Colbert interview that's mostly about how you bring a two-person horse costume everywhere you

---

[47] Van Horn, Caitlin. "Four Wedding Traditions, From the Garter Toss to the Color of Your Gown, Explained." *Brides*. 5 November 2013. https://www.brides.com/story/history-of-wedding-traditions

travel[48]. Is it more feminist to diet or wear Spanx? What was I talking about? Oh right, finding the perfect wedding dress!

Bridal dress samples generally come in size 8-12 in bridal sizes, meaning they're size 6-10 in regular "street" sizes. This makes no sense, but it's just always been that way, like Daylight Savings time and male presidents. Consultants will use clips to help you see what the dress will look like when it's properly altered for your size. It's a weird system that requires some imagination, but a good consultant can guide you through it.

Bridal salons generally carry some plus-sized samples, but I recommend calling ahead to find out how many. What sucks is that nearly every designer MAKES dresses in plus sizes, but you won't be able to try them all on. (The brides I know weren't comfortable ordering dresses they couldn't see on their bodies.) I'd hate for you to get to a store and only find four samples you can try on.

Some plus-size ladies have also reported size discrimination from consultants. I wish this weren't the case, but bridal is slowly becoming more inclusive. One of my plus-size friends had three good experiences at three different stores in L.A., New York City and Buffalo. Search Yelp reviews for "plus" or "curvy" to read accounts from other plus-size ladies and look out for specifically plus-size trunk shows. For links to specific plus-size brands and stores, see the appendix.

If possible, go dress shopping on a weekday, when salons are less busy and you'll get more attention. "I went by myself for the first time on a Monday and there was no one there," says Takla.

You might also want to avoid holiday weekends, when many brides shop with friends and family members who visit from out of town. Bridal appointments generally last 60-90 minutes, but you might be able to stay longer at an empty salon.

One salon I visited only let my friend try on four dresses and then made us leave, even though there were no other customers. Weird, right? You might want to ask over the phone if the store has any such rules. Some stores also forbid you from taking photos. I think the owners are worried that you'll photograph a dress and then go buy it somewhere else or have a tailor make a knock-off. One store I visited asked brides to only photograph their top three favorites, a policy that actually ended up making the appointment more efficient – you don't necessarily want a photo shoot of a bunch of dresses you're definitely not going to buy. Or maybe you do. You do you!

Not every bride will have an emotional moment while buying a dress. Some brides cry because staring at themselves in a wedding dress makes them realize that they're ACTUALLY GETTING MARRIED! WOO! But plenty of brides just think, "Yep, I look hot, take my Visa" and then go rage on

---

[48] Check it out: https://www.youtube.com/watch?v=SpA49ZgOeAM

cheesecake. If you love a dress but don't cry, it doesn't mean you shouldn't buy the thing. If you're not someone who likes clothes, then it makes sense that you wouldn't get all John Boehner about a dress. Don't force yourself to try on a zillion gowns because you haven't wept. Some brides really do end up picking the first dress or only visiting one store.

Now, for the dolla dolla billz. If you want to spend less than $1,000, if you're obsessed with bargains or if you want a nontraditional gown, consider the following options:

Shop a trunk show.

During a trunk show, a designer's representative will bring all dresses from the designer's current collection to a store so you can try them all on – and snag a discount such as 10% off. When it's not hosting a trunk show, a store might only carry a handful of a designer's dresses even though it's an authorized retailer of the brand. Check online for schedules. Also be aware that you'll have to BUY your dress during the trunk show to get the discount, so you might need to do a few shopping outings first.

FYI, Takla says she didn't have a good trunk show experience because her consultant only showed her dresses from the trunk show designer. "I only got to try on four dresses in two hours and the consultant tried to convince me to go with the trunk show designer because of the discount – but it was only 10-12% off, which doesn't matter if the dresses are double your budget," she says. "Just say no and speak up! Make sure the consultant knows if you're interested in more than just the trunk show designer."

Keep your eye on sales.

Stores like David's Bridal and BHLDN will cut prices at some point. Sizes are often limited when dresses get majorly discounted, but perhaps you'll be lucky! Also, David's has many regular-price dresses under $1,000. My sister got a gorgeous, new-collection, regular-price dress there for only $599! If you don't want an elaborate style, it should be even easier to stay in budget.

Buy a preowned dress.

PreOwnedWeddingDresses.com, for example, has a TON of options in a variety of styles, designers, styles and price ranges. This is also a great option if you love the idea of getting a $10,000 dress for $5,000 instead of a new $5,000 dress. Just read return policies VERY carefully; many of the dresses are final sale, so you might not want to buy one unless you A) have already tried that dress on in a store, B) are decisive and VERY confident you know how the shape will look on your body or C) are able to go to the seller's house to try it on (some will let you do this). Also, be sure to buy a dress that's your size or a bit larger – a dress can usually be taken out one size, but not more than that. And if it's huge on you, alterations could be expensive.

Buy a sample.

Salons sell off their old samples, so if you are sample-sized or smaller, you can get a deal buying a last-season dress – just know that samples might have some wear and tear or discoloration (beading can turn dark from oxidation). You can also visit discount bridal stores that exclusively sell samples, like Vows Bridal Outlet in Boston, featured in the short-lived show *I Found the Gown.* (What happened to that show?? I miss those accents! Are the adorable owners still married? Dare I Google it?) You can also find samples for sale online at sites like YourDreamDress.com.

Buy a non-bridal gown.

If you search online for white or ivory floor-length dresses that aren't specifically bridal gowns, I think you'll be surprised at how many gorgeous and affordable ones you'll find. (This is admittedly easier for brides who wear street size 0-12.) Even if you'd never buy a sweater at a luxury store like Neiman Marcus, its dresses might still be in your budget because they're not made-to-order gowns, and many stores will have sales or promo codes. Many also offer free returns, so there's no risk if you don't like the dress - just read any Final Sale warnings carefully. Check out the following stores:

<u>**Both physical and online stores:**</u>
- Bloomingdales
- Lane Bryant
- Neiman Marcus
- Neiman Marcus Last Call
- Nordstrom
- Nordstrom Rack
- Saks Fifth Avenue
- Saks Off Fifth
- Barneys New York
- Barneys Warehouse

<u>**Online-only stores:**</u>
- The Outnet
- Asos
- Modcloth
- Revolve
- ShopBop
- Bluefly
- Lulus

I have bought items from all these stores and sites (I have a problem! Thank you for buying this book!), so I can vouch that they're real stores that sell authentic merchandise. Be wary of sketchy brands with pretty Instagram ads or Pinterest pins but suspicious websites; you might end up with a dress that looks nothing like the photo and no way of getting a refund. Check Yelp reviews or Better Business Bureau ratings if you're unsure. If something seems too good to be true, like a fully beaded ball gown for $100, it probably is.

Have a dress custom-made

Although "custom" might sound like "$$$$," many local seamstresses can make you a one-of-a-kind dress for a very reasonable price. A friend of mine longed for a 1950s-style, cocktail-length gown and chose different elements that were customized into one dress that cost under $1,000. Check Yelp and Etsy.

Consider an ivory bridesmaid dress.

Why is it that an A-line chiffon bridal gown is often $1,000 and an A-line chiffon bridesmaid dress is $200? I feel like ivory bridesmaids dresses are the biggest bargain secret of the wedding dress world, especially if you don't like trains or are looking for something simple or beachy. When you buy a bridesmaid dress at a traditional bridal salon, it works the same way as when you buy a bridal gown: you'll try on a sample and custom-order a dress that will arrive in a few months. But most bridesmaid dresses generally cost $150-$300, so even if you buy a high-end bridesmaid dress, you'll still be spending less than many brides. If you're worried that people might be able to tell that your gown is a bridesmaid dress, I'd avoid the most common style: a strapless or thick-strapped A-line, chiffon, natural-waist gown. To look less like a typical bridesmaid, check out dropped-waist, mermaid or fit-and-flare styles, tulle dresses, satin dresses and sequined or lace designs. You can also add a belt or sash – and if you wear a veil or headpiece, you'll definitely look like a bride. I love Allure Bridesmaids style 1507 and think it could absolutely be a bride's gown. I've also personally tried on and loved Impression Bridal Style 20218. See the appendix for more.

Rent or borrow a dress.

Did you know that Rent the Runway carries wedding gowns? You can rent one for under $100 and still wear a designer dress. Other local stores also offer dress rentals. Rentals can be great options for rehearsal dinners, bachelorette parties and engagement parties, too. The only downside of renting a dress is that you won't be able to get it altered.

You could also ask to borrow a dress from a friend or family member – but don't forget to budget for alterations. "I wore my Mom's dress and thought that would save money but NOPE," Kait says.

Finally, have fun dress shopping! When else do you get to wear a red carpet-esque gown? If the answer is "all the time because I'm a super fancy celebrity," please know that I am totes available for plus-one duties.

Chapter Nineteen

BRIDESMAID DRESSES, TUXES AND SUITS

Why is it common for bridesmaids to buy dresses while groomsmen (and grooms) often rent tuxedos or suits? This makes even less sense because men might actually wear their tuxedo or suit again, while women usually can't wear their bridesmaid dresses twice. The patriarchy prevails!!

Economics student Jennifer Dulski explored this topic in one of her class papers, positing that women are more likely than men to want to make a fashion statement on big social occasions.[49] Because of that, she theorizes, dress rental stores would have to carry a larger variety of styles, while a tuxedo or suit rental shop could carry just a handful of classic styles. To keep up with fashion trends, the store would have to change its inventory of dresses more often than its inventory of suits and tuxes, making dresses more expensive to rent - perhaps even more expensive than buying.

I don't know if I believe this, especially because many classic bridesmaid dress styles have endured for decades. Let's be real, not everyone is rocking two-piece midriff bridesmaid dresses or velvet jumpsuits. It's definitely the patriarchy!!

The good news is that plenty of new options for bridesmaid dresses have sprung up in the last few years. The bad news: bridesmaid dress shopping is a hellscape of insecurities and body issues. Thanks again, patriarchy. "Picking a bridesmaid dress is harder than picking your own wedding dress," one bridal salon owner told me — and she turned out to be right! First off, make sure you have enough time. Start shopping for bridesmaid dresses around six months ahead of your wedding date.

---

[49] Frank, Robert. "Why Do Brides Buy Dresses While Grooms Rent Tuxes?" *PBS News Hour. 1 July 2009.* https://www.pbs.org/newshour/economy/why-do-brides-buy-dresses-whil

The most traditional choice is to put your Maid of Honor and bridesmaids all in the same dress. Apparently, this practice began back in Ancient Roman times, when brides AND bridesmaids would wear the same dress to confuse any evil spirits who might come a-knockin'. It's a little crazy that we still uphold a tradition from people who also gave women the female version of their father's name – even if that meant you and your eight sisters would all be Cornelia – but some traditions are hard to break.[50] Matching bridesmaid dresses also create a kind of unity in photographs, and some people believe they help ensure the bride stands out.

What complicates this is that women come in all shapes and sizes. If your maids have different body types, it's unlikely that they'll all look and feel their best in the same dress. Please also keep in mind that not all colors compliment all skin tones. My friend once had to wear a metallic seafoam green bridesmaid gown, which completely washed her out. She decided to use self-tanner, then woke up the morning of the wedding with orange stripes all across her shoulders. She called her mom in a panic and they were able to spray her whitest parts to even her out, but we can all learn some lessons here: 1) don't self-tan right before bed; 2) maybe don't self-tan at all unless your BFF is there to spray your naked self for you, like usual; 3) thank goodness for moms; and 4) Nordic blondes and part-Asian brunettes feel confident in different shades.

In the past, many brides have said "Too bad!" to the idea that their bridesmaids should like their bridesmaid dresses. But since you're a cool, modern feminist who values female friendships, you actually care about how your friends feel. If you do want to choose one single bridesmaid dress style, opt for forgiving silhouettes and fabrics, such as an A-line chiffon gown. If your maids have vastly different body types than you do, you might ask them what shapes they like or go through their social media photos to see for yourself.

Straps (or strap options) might also be a good idea, especially if you have busty maids. Most strapless dresses come with detachable spaghetti straps, and you could also allow your maids to order extra fabric to create thicker straps for more bust support. My best friend's cousin did this with tulle and looked great – and since the rest of her dress was the same as our strapless dresses, we all looked uniform.

Another option is to choose the color, fabric, length (and brand, if you want totally uniform colors) of the bridesmaid dress and then let your maids choose the style. A mix of straps, strapless, one-shoulder, etc. can be fun. You could also pick a convertible dress that can be worn multiple ways, such as one from Two Birds or David's Bridal. Note: if you're choosing different

---

[50] The Romans also invented satire and public health, so I guess they weren't completely terrible.

dresses within the same brand, have everyone order the dresses at the same time through the same store so that they all come from the same dye lot.

If you'd like variety in your bridesmaid dresses, you can put your maids in different shades of a color or even choose multiple colors that go together. (Dusty rose, grey and lavender are a pretty mix, for example; various shades of blue are also lovely). Coordinating multiple colors and shades definitely takes a bit of work, though. If five maids choose a dark navy dress and one chooses a sky blue one, the group might look weird. Get some internet inspiration and make sure your maids have very clear instructions. If you're staying within the same base color but letting maids choose different brands, remember that some colors will pose more of a challenge. Different black or navy gowns might blend together more easily than magenta or red ones.

To control a collection of mismatched dresses, you could pick 5-20 specific dresses and have your maids send you their top three picks. Then you could assign a dress and/or color to each person – and if two maids have the same top choice, make them fight over it!! Or let the first responder have it.

If you let maids shop on their own, tell them if you want them to send you photos for confirmation before they purchase. If you tell your maids "pick whatever" and then are unhappy with the results, you might have to foot the bill to replace expensive, un-returnable dresses.

It is generally standard to ask your bridesmaids to pay for their dresses – and it's a good idea to keep your friends' and family members' budgets in mind. "The worst part of being a bridesmaid is being asked to wear an ugly, expensive dress," says Colorado Lauren, who was once asked to wear a "shit-brown" dress in a family wedding. But even if you choose a flattering style and color, it's unlikely that a bridesmaid will wear the dress again – so choose a price point that makes sense based on this.

Also remember that base dress costs don't include the price of alterations, shipping or tax. (If you fall in love with a dress that's above your price target, you might want to cover the costs of shipping or tax.) Try to put yourself in your maids' shoes. If you've been a bridesmaid yourself, you can think back to how you felt and what you thought was a reasonable budget. Also, be up front with your bridesmaids about the fact that you expect them to buy a dress if they've never been in a wedding party before.

Why do many bridesmaid dresses cost $250 when some department store evening gowns in the same fabric only cost $120?? That's right, it's the patriarchy!! Actually, I think it's a classic case of capitalism; brands and stores know that as soon as they categorize something as wedding-related, they can charge more because society has taught us to seek out that perfect dream wedding. But it also has to do with the special-ordering discussed in the previous chapter. With most bridesmaid dresses, maids will visit a bridal or special-occasion salon, try on a sample size and then order a gown in the right size. These are non-returnable; if the dresses don't fit perfectly, maids can get alterations.

If looking at sample gowns on your maids is important to you, you can all shop together – but this can be a challenge if your maids live in different cities or have busy schedules. One of my friends found that organizing a shopping trip was a much bigger headache than she anticipated.

Another option is to go shopping with just one or two local maids and choose a dress style for everyone based on how they look. You can also ask your maids to visit their local salon to try on a sample and then send you a photo before you make a choice. Just check brand websites and call salons to confirm that your maids will be able to try on a sample of the right dress. As with wedding gowns, many stores only carry particular samples as opposed to the brand's entire collection.

A few online stores, such as Azazie and Kennedy Blue, offer the same salon procedure (gowns made to order) at a lower price because they don't have brick-and-mortar shops. Both brands will mail you free or low-priced swatches; they'll also send you samples to try at home, but these are generally not free.

If you're looking to spend less than what bridesmaid dresses cost at bridal salons, you can choose a dress from a website or department store that isn't specifically a bridesmaid dress. This is admittedly harder if members of your bridal party are plus-sized, but for example, I am currently considering a $89 gown from Lulus, and it's just as nice as many $180 dresses I've tried on. I've also seen inexpensive dress options at Asos, Amazon and others - and since these aren't made-to-order, they're returnable. If you have a small bridal party, it might be easy to find a non-bridesmaid dress that works for everyone this way.

My sister decided to let her bridesmaids choose any dress that has some skirt movement and is A) floor-length, B) solid navy, C) not shiny and D) not fully beaded. There are plenty out there for under $100! I could also get a deal on a second-hand dress or rent a dress that fits her criteria from a site like Vow to Be Chic or Rent the Runway. See the appendix for more sites!

Knee-length dresses tend to be cheaper than long ones, but short dresses mean you'll be able to see your maids' shoes – so if you're picky about shoes, your maids might not save money after all.

Finally, let go of the idea that your bridesmaids are going to be able to wear the dress again. Listen to Katherine Heigl in *27 Dresses*.[51] My friend once wore a long, black curve-hugging gown as a bridesmaid and then wore it again when I took her as a plus-one to the American Music Awards, where I was required to continually live-tweet about some Nokia phone (I've done some

---

[51] Yes, I'm a feminist and I like that movie. It's legitimately good, and I'd be happy to argue about this with you on Twitter - @amandapendo.

weird crap in my career). She looked great, but a catty mom sized her up in the ladies room and told her straight to her face, "Too fancy." (WTF!) I guess the lesson there is that you really can't wear bridesmaid dresses again. And that women in the bathroom at the AMAs are as harsh as Nina Garcia on unconventional materials day.

Now let's talk about grooms (and brides who don't like dresses)! For the most formal look, opt for tuxedos. However, many grooms pick suits in black, grey, brown or tan. Grooms can rent or buy, while it's most common for Best Men and groomsmen to rent. As with bridesmaid dresses, you can rent from a local store or an online-only version. Shop early if you're looking for a color or material that will be out of season in the final months leading up to your wedding.

"I bought a tux for my wedding," says Sam. "It turned out it's very hard in L.A. to find a tux in the summer/fall, unless you want a linen tux. But these days, it seems like grooms are doing suits, which give you more options than tuxes. Grooms buy a nice suit and then it becomes their main suit to wear to other things after the wedding. (Although I've gotten to wear my tux a few times since then because I'm a very fancy person.)"

Another bride told me that her now-hubby chose to buy a custom-made suit. Since then, it's become his go-to suit for all special occasions. A new suit can be a good investment if you know you'll be attending a lot of weddings after yours. Or if you're a Very Fancy Person™.

The groom can decide to match perfectly with his Best Man and groomsmen, or he can stand out with a different colored tux or suit. Sam wore navy while his groomsmen wore black, for example; I've also seen grooms wear navy while their groomsmen wore grey. "To make them match better, we did shawl collars for both," Sam says.

A groom could also differentiate himself by wearing a bowtie, a tie in a different color, or a tie in a different pattern. Check Pinterest for even more ideas! I've even seen a groom in grey pants amid some bold groomsmen in maroon pants. Go nuts!

Grooms can also stand out in photographs by leaving their suit jackets on while the groomsmen take theirs off. (Your photographer will have other good ideas in this vein.) Plus, nobody will be confused about who the groom is because he'll be smiling beatifically, basking in the fact that he convinced you, THE COOLEST, SMARTEST, HOTTEST WOMAN EVER, to hang out with him literally forever.

You can further personalize the dudes' look (and coordinate with the bridesmaids) by choosing ties, bowties, vests, suspenders and pocket squares. Boutonnieres – flowers worn in the lapel – will also tie your color scheme together. For a more casual look, you can ask the groomsmen to wear sneakers; funky, colorful socks and/or sunglasses can also make for memorable photos.

Sam had his dudes rent tuxes from online rental store The Black Tux, which he was happy with, especially given that his groomsmen had a variety of builds (BTW, another groom also recommended The Black Tux to me). Sam admits that their products aren't the cheapest options on the market, but he thinks they're worth it.

"Definitely don't do the cheapest rental tux," Sam says. "You think you're doing your groomsmen a favor by saving them money, but they fit terribly. The pants are basically parachute pants, and everyone looks goofy."

Choose the groomsmen's attire after you choose the bridesmaid dresses. A general rule of thumb is to start shopping for tuxes four to six months before the wedding. If some or all of the groomsmen are local, you can schedule a group fitting for a fun bonding experience. If men live out of town, they can visit any tux rental shop, get their measurements taken and call the store where the groom is ordering all the tuxes. Or, if you're using a national chain like Men's Wearhouse, you could have the groomsmen rent from their local store. One bride told me that her only Bridezilla moment came when rented suits were not ready when they were supposed to be (just ten days before the wedding). Even if you delegate suit rental to your groom, you might need to stay on top of such things. Luckily, the bride's stern phone call worked and the suits were ready for the wedding.

The Man Registry recommends telling your groomsmen what specific pieces and accessories they need – cufflinks, cummerbunds, shoes, etc.[52] A good general rule is to provide detailed instructions for both groomsmen and bridesmaids. You might also want to give bridal party members fake early deadlines to account for procrastinators. We all have that friend who kills at beer pong but has literally never been on time.

---

[52] Easter, Chris. "Wedding Tuxedo Rental Tips." *The Man Registry.* 1 Dec 2011. https://themanregistry.com/groom-101/wedding-tuxedo-rental-tips/

Chapter Twenty

BACHELOR AND BACHELORETTE PARTIES

It's here! The day you've been dreaming of since you were a little girl! You finally get to drink a 27-dollar vodka soda while a shirtless *Magic Mike Live* dancer smashes his obliques into your face!

Well, if that's your thing. You don't have to get drunk or go to a strip club just because they're common traditions. "Hated every minute of it," says one groom from the UK. Tell the members of your bridal party what you do and don't want! They might think that taking you to a strip club is their obligation - but it doesn't have to be.

Also, you might have to explicitly tell your Maid of Honor or Best Man that you expect him/her to plan a bachelorette or bachelor party, if you want one. One bride told me that her younger sister was her Maid of Honor and didn't think to plan anything.

If you DON'T want a party at all, that's fine too. "Those seem like a morose funeral for singlehood," says Deirdre, who was happy with her decision to forego a bachelorette party.

The groom from New Mexico also skipped the bachelor party. "I refuse to do things just because they are expected," he says. (See, some people already embrace YOU DO YOU as a life motto.)

But if you want a bachelorette or bachelor party, you've got plenty of options. It doesn't have to include scantily-clad dancers or ill-advised tequila shots. Rent a house on a lake and sit around making s'mores if you need to chill the fuck out amid wedding planning! Have fun and let the party be an opportunity for your friends and family members to get to know each other better. This can help wedding mingling!

If your friends all live in different cities, you might opt for a full weekend, but if you're all in the same place, a single, informal day or night outing can be just as fun. In fact, it might be *easier* to have fun if you're not putting some kind of unrealistic New Year's Eve-type pressure on a long weekend. You also don't need to spend a ton of money to have fun.

Some bachelor/bachelorette ideas:

- Wine tour
- Brewery tour
- Distillery tour
- Pub crawl
- Beer, wine or food festival
- Bike rental or tour
- Skiing/snowboarding/tubing
- Lake or beach house rental
- Camping
- Hiking
- Fishing
- Massages, facials, mani-pedis
- Poker or other card games
- Casino trip
- Board games
- Concert
- Musical or play
- Comedy show
- Sporting event
- Boat rental
- Kayaking
- Surfing
- Paddle-boarding
- White-water rafting
- Outdoor picnic
- Afternoon tea
- Fondue
- Escape room
- Murder mystery party
- Painting or pottery class
- Cooking or baking class
- Video game competition
- DIY crafting
- Car show
- Luxury car rental
- Off-roading tour
- Medieval Times/Ren Faire
- Safari or zoo trip
- Mixology class

- Pole dancing class
- Salsa dancing class
- Hot air balloon ride
- Skydiving
- Parasailing
- Bungee jumping
- Amusement park
- Trampoline park
- Gun range
- Archery class
- Group fitness class
- Golfing
- Go-Karting
- Paintball
- Laser tag
- Rock climbing
- Nostalgic slumber party
- Bowling
- Ice skating
- Holiday outing (like Halloween)
- Sex toy party
- Makeup, hair or fragrance party

Some couples also like to combine their bachelor/bachelorette parties into a modern, co-ed party or shower. It definitely changes the dynamic, but it's not as though you were going to spend the night making out with strangers anyway. (…Right?)

If you're planning a bachelorette or bachelor party, start by choosing a date and putting together your guest list. It's common to invite people who aren't in the bridal party, but don't go insane. Even though some people will decline the invite, you don't need to invite 30 people. You're already planning a wedding – let your bachelorette or bachelor party be more fun and relaxing.

The more people you invite, the more complicated things can get – especially if people don't all get along. "My bridal party *Mean Girl'd* another bridesmaid," says Anastasiya. "I had a falling out with one of my best friends, and we didn't speak for two years. But we reconciled before the wedding. My friends from home wouldn't allow her to come to my bachelorette party because they couldn't believe that we had reconciled after the way she had acted. The situation was complicated, but it put a damper on the celebration. In the end, I just had to put up with it and ask my friend not to come to the bachelorette party." She says it worked out in the end, but "it made the wedding day festivities awkward since everyone sort of avoided each other."

I personally found that offering people too many options or asking questions made the party planning process more stressful. I recommend being decisive and essentially telling people, "This is how it's going to be, come or don't come." Also give people firm deadlines for when they need to RSVP or make other decisions. You'll still have to chase some people, but people respond best to specific deadlines. (I'm super fun to make plans with.) I tried to make it clear that I wasn't pressuring anyone to attend – I just wanted an answer – and they seemed to understand.

If you're comfortable with it, you can outsource most of the planning to your Maid of Honor or Best Man. If you want to be surprised, they'll probably be cool with that! Just let them know what kind of vibe you're looking for and how much you want to spend or ask others to spend. Also, be up front about whether you want no strippers, no hard drugs, no plastic penis items, no actual live human penises, etc. If you're super lame and un-fun, that's fine. Kidding! All the plastic penis items totally weird me out. Even if marriage means you're about to see one for the first time, why all the quasi-edgy ceremonial plasticware?

If you're a control freak, it's okay if you want to do the majority of the planning for your bachelor/bachelorette party. Just be up front about that! Asking people to plan a party and then micromanaging them is apparently not the best way to maintain friendships.

Next, the planner should pick a party location and do some internet searching about potential dates to make sure that Vegas isn't already popping with UFC fights and dentist conventions[53]. I sent group emails to lock in the date that worked best for the most people BEFORE I checked on these things; if I could do it over again, I'd probably research costs before offering people potential dates. This might not matter if you're going to an inexpensive destination, though.

Keep in mind that if you and your soon-to-be-spouse go on bachelor/bachelorette weekends at different times, it will cancel out two weekends during which you could finish wedding planning stuff together (final meetings, conference calls, etc.). It's not the end of the world, but one bride I know wanted to make sure that she and her fiancé weren't unavailable for two separate weekends.

One of the hardest parts of throwing a successful bachelor/bachelorette party is entertaining people with very different personalities and lifestyles. Your conservative cousin might not enjoy the same things as crazy Dana from work. Try to be accommodating – but you also have to let go a little. The most important thing is whether the bride or groom is having a good time, and everyone who attends the party knows and accepts this. You can't

---

[53] I know from experience that UFC fights and dentist conventions raise the costs of hotel rooms and airfare!

please everyone, and I honestly should have spent a lot less time at *Magic Mike Live* wondering if the eight months-pregnant bridesmaid was feeling scandalized by the dude dancing all up on her. She was fine. She was the one who brought a giant blow-up penis to our hotel room! I should have had another 27-dollar vodka soda.

Games can be a way to bring together people who don't know each other well. At two different bachelorette parties, I brought mad libs for everyone to fill out and they ended up being a big hit. You can find some online, but if you're an egomaniacal writer like I am, you'll decide after using one internet mad lib that you can write a better one yourself. I've also seen pre-packaged bachelorette games like "what's in the bride's purse" or "who knows the bride best," but I feel like A) maybe the bride doesn't want to talk about her hemorrhoid cream and B) it's weird to get your friends together and make them compete for the title of BFF. But check Party City and Amazon for game options!

You don't necessarily have to stay wedding-themed in your activities. You can play games like Cards Against Humanity, Never Have I Ever and Exploding Kittens. You can also make up some kind of scavenger hunt to get the bride or groom to talk to strangers. At one bachelorette I attended, the bride had fun trying to get photos with various men. We ended up accepting a man-bun for "Man with a ponytail" and a mannequin for "Man in uniform". What can I say, San Diego is not a hugely populated Man-city. The overall point is that you should be creative! Sometimes these free activities create the best bachelor and bachelorette memories – and your guests will be thrilled to save some money.

In fact, party attendees' biggest complaint is generally the price. Try to be up-front about what things will cost. Discuss if people plan to pay for the bride's or groom's meals, drinks, etc. If you're asking people to pay for transportation and lodging somewhere, I think it's best not to ask them to spend additional money to buy gifts or cover the guest of honor's expenses. But if you're staying in town, it can be a nice gesture to pay for the bride's or groom's dinner or drinks.

You could also agree not to buy gifts or all chip in a few bucks for one gift instead of asking everyone to buy something (especially since people will also be buying wedding gifts and in some cases, a shower gift). At one bachelorette I attended, we played a fun game in which we all bought the bride lingerie and had her guess who bought what – but this was a local weekend that didn't require us to purchase flights. Be mindful of how much things are adding up. The most important thing, though, is that you don't spring a bunch of costs on guests after they've agreed to attend. Give estimates ahead of time so that people can make smart decisions based on their budgets.

Guests also tend to get angry if they're asked to pay for things they didn't use. It's reasonable to ask guests to split the cost of snacks or cups, but you shouldn't ask a pregnant or sober person to split the cost of the group's alcohol. I'm also not a fan of splitting dinners evenly unless people order similarly priced items and have agreed to an even split ahead of time. At my best friend's bachelorette, I put all dinners on my credit card, had everyone initial their items on the receipt and then emailed them later to charge them for exactly what they ordered. This took a bit of math and might be too annoying for you, but either way, I recommend having a dinner payment plan before you walk in and order lobster like you're the carpet king of Wisconsin. You could also ask everyone to bring cash – just make sure you give them enough time to hit the ATM.

Keep track of who's paying for Lyfts, parking fees or other costs if you split things up later. Having one person pay for everything can be easy; you can also assign different costs to different people ahead of time. Save receipts when you can. You'll thank me when it's the morning after six shots of SoCo and you can't remember why you're getting texts from "Adam Brooklyn Gym Teacher," much less the cost of onion rings.

"I went to a bachelorette where the Maid of Honor charged everyone an estimated base price for everything ahead of time," says a bride from Santa Monica, CA. "Afterward, based on the final costs, she asked for more money or gave a refund, depending on the person. It worked well." This can be a good option if nobody has a credit card with a high enough limit to cover everything.

If you want to give your guests favors, there are plenty of fun ideas on Pinterest and Etsy. You can buy and take fun photos with personalized tank tops/t-shirts, tattoos, tote bags, visors, hats, sunglasses, cups and more. Generic necklaces, shot glasses and the like (check out Party City) are also fun and a little less expensive than personalized items; you can also get custom stickers made and put them on cheap, plain items such as cups.

It can be easy to get swept up in all this crap, though; don't feel pressured to buy everything. If you're the bride or groom, you may want to tell your party organizer if you do or do not want certain items. Personalized tank tops are fun, but it's likely you won't ever wear them again – hence why I went for "Rosé all day" tank tops instead of personalized ones when I planned my best friend's bachelorette. OBVI, rosé will still be worth celebrating even when everybody's old and married.

Good communication between attendees can also help stem the tide of bachelor/bachelorette accessories. Bridal party members might separately buy a bunch of things if they don't know who's bringing what.

Don't you dare stick to a low-carb diet on your bachelorette! You will thank me later. Also, stock up on water, Gatorade and maybe even hangover vitamins; my friends and I all tested out Drinkwel vitamins and felt like they did make a difference. Otherwise, you might need to pay $99 to get in a random van and go to a strip mall off the Vegas strip so that someone who claims to be a doctor can give you an IV of saline solution while you watch *The Hangover* on a TV with the motion smoothing turned on[54].

Take lots of photos and videos! I will always cherish the video in which my best friend apologizes to me for chugging half a bottle of rosé because strangers dared her. She knew I'd disapprove – but I guess it's my fault for buying her a tank top that said "Rosé all day."

---

[54] No, Mom, I've definitely never done this.

Chapter Twenty-One

GIFT REGISTRIES AND SHOWERS

One of your guests has to be rich enough to buy you a Le Creuset Dutch oven, right? Or at LEAST a hot-ass turquoise KitchenAid mixer. Point is, a wedding registry allows you to tell guests exactly which gifts you'd like and ensures that they don't purchase duplicate items.

You might be surprised by how early guests will ask about your registry. One bride told me that she hadn't even picked out a venue when relatives started inquiring. Turns out they wanted to buy her engagement presents! Not exactly the worst problem to have, STACEY. If your relatives are less aggressive about this, you might be able to make registry decisions much later.

One bride I spoke with asked only for cash and gift cards, since cash is a traditional wedding gift in China and she wanted to stick to her family's cultural tradition. But another bride said that when she wanted to ask for only gift cards at her shower (not even her wedding) because she'd need to take all the presents on a plane, her mother wouldn't let her. Customs vary by culture and region.

If you do create a registry, remember that some guests really want to buy physical gifts; some also want to be able to go into a store and look at items, so you might want to set up a registry with at least one store that still has physical locations. There's no real limit to how many stores you can register at. Have fun with that barcode scanner zappy thing! Just make sure you put links to each of your registries on your wedding website (many wedding website templates make importing this information easy).

Set your shipping address as a place where you'll be ready to receive gifts early on. Unattended gifts might be stolen by the same chick who stole the vegan leather jacket[55] I ordered myself on Christmas and didn't know would arrive Dec 27th, when I was still out of town. Who knew that Zara is so quick! Who knew that detectives from the Santa Monica police department leave you voicemails saying, "No, I really am a detective. You can look it up."

Check each store's return and exchange policy before you commit. Many stores let you return items for store credit, so even if you don't really want a registry but a relative is making you get one, you might end up with some useful gift cards later.

Traditionally, common registry items include anything related to the home: dishes, frying pans, towels, sheets, furniture, vacuums, etc. Check out The Knot's exhaustive checklist for more ideas. However, wedding registries have changed a lot over the years, especially since many engaged couples already live together. Don't feel like you have to put fancy kitchen items on your registry just because they pop up first on store websites.

Eleven years after her wedding, Cambria Bold at *The Kitchn* says that she still uses her dishes, flatware, cookware, wine glasses and mini food processor, but she rarely takes out her wine decanter, napkin rings, panini press, multi-piece plastic utensil set, 15-piece knife block and bread machine.[56] She also recommends registering for an instant-read thermometer, a good chef's knife, a pepper mill, a strong blender, an electric kettle, beautiful bakeware, half sheet pans, a pressure cooker and an enameled Dutch oven (Le Creuset, you will be mine someday). But maybe you wouldn't use these things! If you don't cook, or if you already own all the kitchen items you need, register for other crap instead. Be honest about how much cooking, baking and entertaining you do. Sure, it sounds fun to sous-vide your food, but will you actually cook with weird plastic pouches? Remember the way you ghosted your vegetable spiralizer?! Today's InstantPot is tomorrow's panini press. Marriage isn't going to magically turn you into Bobby Flay.

Talk to your partner about items you'd both enjoy. Here are some less-traditional ideas:

- Luggage or other travel items
- Camping gear
- Backyard, patio or pool items
- Grill or grill accessories
- Tools

---

[55] Can't "vegan leather" be literally anything? Like, here's a vegan leather jacket made out of old diapers!

[56] Bold, Cambria. "The Wedding Registry Gifts We Still Use 10 Years Later (and the Ones We Don't)." *The Kitchn*. 12 May 2017. https://www.thekitchn.com/the-5-kitchen-wedding-registry-gifts-we-still-use-10-years-later-and-those-we-dont-life-in-the-kitchen-219902

- Gardening equipment
- Board games or card games
- Organizational or space-saving items
- Home office or desk supplies
- Artwork or other wall decor
- Workout or sporting equipment
- Personalized or monogrammed items
- Tablets, speakers or other electronics
- Smart thermostat or doorbell
- Home security system
- Fancy garbage can[57]
- Seasonal/holiday items
- Mattress
- Air purifier or humidifier
- Pet accessories
- Safety equipment (fire extinguisher, carbon monoxide detector, etc.)

To give your guests plenty of options, choose gifts at a variety of price points. Register for the must-haves first, then track what you receive and add second-tier items later on. You don't want to register for so much that you don't get the basics – but we've all been that person who logs onto a registry at the last minute and only finds a $5 spatula and a $500 juicer. It's the worst!

Finally, make sure you include some whimsical gifts – anything from a neon green ice cream scoop to a decorative wooden giraffe – amid practical things like plates. Uncle Herman might not be a plate guy.

Sites such as Zola, Honeyfund and The Knot's Newlywed Fund offer ways to put honeymoon items and other nontraditional things on your registry. For example, you can have guests send you money that will go toward a plane ticket, hotel stay or tourist activity. Some couples worry that these kinds of sites are tacky, but I've enjoyed using them. I loved buying my friends tickets to a museum in France; when they returned from their honeymoon, they wrote about their experience in their thank you note, and I didn't feel like I'd sent them an impersonal chunk of cash.

You can also register for funds toward services or classes that might be useful in your marriage – anything that might make your life easier. Here are some ideas:

- Housecleaning service
- Plow service
- Lawn mowing or landscaping service

---

[57] One day, I will be fancy enough for a stainless steel, no-touch garbage can. One day.

- Car washes or oil changes
- Dry cleaning
- Meal delivery service
- Wine, coffee, cheese or other club
- Grooming or beauty subscription
- Entertainment subscription
- Cooking class
- Sewing class
- Gym membership
- Massage
- Facial
- Haircut or blowout
- Counseling session
- Financial planning or tax prep session
- Home improvements or repairs

Zola offers links to some specific services like these; for example, on Zola, you can register for a blowout at Drybar. But you could also fill in your own local vendor or list a generic "blowout" and have guests send you money through the site.

If you use a cash-item registry site to add your own items/services that aren't already listed (the way Drybar is), guests will be charged around 2-4% in credit card processing fees for each transaction. However, you can absorb this fee if you don't want guests to feel like they have to send you $102.50 for you to receive $100.

You could potentially skip the traditional registry altogether. Many couples have done this and survived! One couple I know requested that wedding guests send them records so they could expand their music collection with an eclectic mix of what their guests enjoyed.[58] You could also ask guests to contribute to your favorite charity in lieu of gifts. The Knot also has a "The Knot Gifts Back" program that donates up to 3% of registry purchases to the charity of your choice.

If you feel guilty about asking guests to buy you gifts at all, you probably haven't been to as many weddings as I have and thus can't relate to "A Woman's Right to Shoes," season 6, episode 9 of *Sex and the City* (watch it after you finish this book!). Still, I applaud your anti-materialism. Just bear in mind that some of your guests really WANT to buy you something and may send you gifts even if you ask them not to. As with every element of your wedding, your registry choice can elicit vocal opinions. If you write on your

---

[58] I'll be honest, though. I thought about sending them an Ellie Goulding record, got mad that the one I found didn't have my favorite song on it, and then sent them a vintage mid-century platter instead.

wedding website that your guests' presence is gift enough, you will still receive some random gifts, some monetary checks and some comments about how only evil demons get married without registries. Stay strong!

Keep in mind that your cousin doesn't buy you frilly napkins because she hates you. She's trying to show her love in the way she knows how. Sometimes you have to let people take care of you. Be polite and don't make harsh demands when it comes to gifts.

Establish your registry in advance of any bridal showers. Traditionally, a relative or Maid of Honor will host a shower for the bride – but feel free to bring this up with your family members or friends if you haven't heard anything. Many brides help with planning, from guest list to location. As the bride, you'll also be the connection between relatives and friends who don't know each other but want to be involved. "My fiance's aunt reached out to me and wanted to host a shower for just his side of the family," says a Buffalo bride. "The concept of having two showers, one for each side, was totally foreign to me." She ultimately put the aunt in touch with her mother so that they could join forces to plan just one shower.

You can also talk with your host about the shower vibe you'd like. That said, shower planning might be another area where you need to let go of control and allow people to take care of you. It's okay! Breathe.

Hosts should send out shower invitations 4-6 weeks ahead of time (2 months for out-of-town guests). Electronic-only invitations are common, but stationery sites offer pretty paper options as well. Put registry information on the invite. Just make sure your host doesn't invite anyone who isn't invited to the wedding!

Don't stress if people can't make it to your shower. If you're asking people to travel long distances for a wedding, a bachelorette party AND a shower, it's reasonable that they might only be able to attend one or two of these events. You could also consider tacking your shower onto a bachelorette weekend; just make sure the timing makes sense for moms, aunts or other relatives who wouldn't be invited to the bachelorette. A friend of mine hosted a lovely shower brunch after her bachelorette so that out-of-town friends could attend both, and I was super proud I wasn't too hungover to dominate a word search while freebasing waffles.

You might also consider having multiple showers in different cities, if you and your friends live in one place but your entire family lives in another. "I always wanted a shower," says a bride who had one shower in Los Angeles and another in Oklahoma. "Where I'm from, it's part of the whole experience."

A shower can be traditional or modern, formal or informal, mimosas or lots of mimosas. Some couples also opt for co-ed showers. YOU DO YOU. If cost is a concern, your host may want to have the shower at someone's house/apartment or a public park. Your host could also serve snacks instead of a full meal. Brides are not expected to pay for any of the shower, but it's also not super cool to make friends or relatives feel OBLIGATED to throw you a lavish party.

There are no real rules when it comes to showers except that they're generally PG. Save the dildos and thongs for your bachelorette party, unless it's a friends-only affair. Some showers have themes, like "Paris" or "nautical" or "Barack and Michelle" (sigh), but themes are optional and should probably be left up to the host.

Games are also an option. Some brides find them cheesy, but they can be a good way to help guests who don't know each other (and may vary in age) interact. Stores like Party City sell pre-packaged shower games; your host could also customize a bingo board, write up trivia questions or print out mad libs, word games or puzzles from the internet. Many games center on the bride's personality or the story of how she met her fiancé, but you don't necessarily have to play a wedding-themed game. Break out Jenga if that's your jam! Usually, the host will award the winner of a game some kind of prize; the host can also give out door prizes (with numbered tickets or numbers under everyone's seats).

If you don't want a shower, that's totally fine. Unless your mom really wants to throw you one. Or your best friend. Or your aunt. Or your fiancé's aunt. If you hate being the center of attention or feel weird about getting gifts, you can resist at your own discretion. But if your relatives are stubborn, you might need to make like Elsa and LET IT GOOOOOO.

Chapter Twenty-Two

HOW TO WRITE A SPEECH

As a Maid of Honor for my best friend, I was asked to give a speech at the reception. I'm not gonna lie: I rocked it. Strangers in the bathroom even complimented me! This felt amazing, and I've had my fair share of Surprisingly Meaningful Drunken Conversations With Women In The Bathroom (just not at the American Music Awards!!). I realize that, as a writer, I have an unfair advantage. However, I think my speech tips can work for any Maid of Honor, Best Man or family member speaking at the reception. If you're the bride or groom, you probably won't have to give many official speeches. But if you'd like to say something at an event – or if you're going to be a MOH or Best Man for someone else – these might help!

Prepare

Why do so many people think that you can get away with an impromptu speech? NONONONO. You'll end up giggling and saying "anyway" a lot – which only serves to highlight that whatever you just said was unnecessary. Only improvise if you're speaking for under thirty seconds and saying something very simple and earnest, like "Thank you all for coming. Cheers to the bride and groom." Maybe I'm being demanding; after all, I believe that you shouldn't bother decorating a cupcake if you can't make it look like it's from *Cake Wars*. (I know! Therapy!) But you can do better. Set aside some time to write something, have a couple people read it and give comments, revise it and then practice it several times.

You don't need to memorize the speech. But even if you do, I recommend that you hold a printed copy of it in front of you at the wedding anyway in case you get nervous, have a brain fart or don't speak until after you've shoved all the Prosecco in your face. And don't read your speech off your phone, because weddings are formal and that's lame. As an elder millennial,

I'm allowed to say this! Also, your battery might die or you might accidentally delete the speech. Finally, speak more slowly than you think you need to!

Choose a theme

Your speech will sound cohesive and polished if you begin with some kind of theme, like a common thread in the couple's relationship, and then return to it at the end. At one wedding I attended, the Best Man gave a speech about how in dating, we always talk about "red flags," but with the bride and groom, it was all "green flags," or the things they had in common. It was adorable and I still remember it years later! You could get more serious with a theme like "devotion" or keep it light with the theme of how a Cowboys fan and a Redskins[59] fan have somehow made it work, establishing the foundation for a successful marriage.

Since my best friend met her husband in person at a bar and then later reconnected with him on a dating app, I incorporated a theme of how much technology has changed in the ten years we've known each other and how these new forms of communication have given me records of everything (Mwahaha).

Consider a classic structure

There's no single accepted format for a speech, but you might begin by explaining how you know the bride or groom, how you met (that story in itself could be the speech!) and how long you've known each other. You can then get into why you're so close, maybe telling a specific story. Then at some point you'll want to incorporate a story about the person they're marrying. What was going on in their lives when they met? Did they meet in a funny or unexpected way? Did you know this person was "the one"? If so, how? What are they like together? My cousin's sister spoke about how the groom special-ordered chocolate in the shape of a brain for Valentine's Day and then went to great lengths to make sure his busy neurosurgeon girlfriend got it on time. It was the perfect detail! You can also talk about how this person has become part of the family, if applicable. You might tell one longer story or a collection of shorter stories.

Be specific

Generalities like "She's my best friend," "She's always had my back" and "I've known her since I was a kid" are nice, but they don't paint a picture for your audience. Instead, say something about the bride or groom that couldn't be said by every other speech writer. "Show, don't tell" is an old writing adage that will serve you well. If your sister bossed you around when you were kids, tell a specific story that demonstrates what she was like. My cousin, who

---

[59] Really? We still have a team called the Redskins?

served as Maid of Honor for the aforementioned neurosurgeon, quoted their mother's journal entry from 1990, in which she wrote, "We are teaching Jacqueline to stand up for herself" and detailed a specific anecdote about how the bride constantly barked orders regarding the tea parties they hosted for their American Girl dolls.

Visuals can also help. The philosophy professor I met on OKCupid gave a Best Man speech the week before I gave my Maid of Honor speech and used posters a la the guy who's in love with Keira Knightley *in Love Actually*. (Apparently, the professor and his BFF unabashedly love that movie because they're modern, emotional men). Fear not, he didn't declare his love for the bride or groom – it morphed into a cute message about how the bride was perfect for her new husband. The creative idea was a hit!

Use old journals, emails and text messages as evidence. Guests laughed when I did a live reading of the text message in which my best friend screenshotted her future husband's photo on a dating app, sent it to friends and asked, "Did one of you make out with this guy? He looks familiar." (SHE had made out with him.) I also read aloud a Gchat in which she said that he had texted her THREE WEEKS after their first makeout and said she wasn't going to respond. "He can suck it," she wrote about the man she's now willing to watch football with.

Keep it appropriate

I got REAL in my MOH speech – but I also asked my friend ahead of time if her conservative relatives would be offended by the phrases "make out" and "suck it". (Luckily, the answer was no.) Still, I kept everything pretty PG, avoiding swear words and discussions of anything too drunken or sexual. You can always talk about those things at the bachelor or bachelorette party! It's fun to lightly tease the bride and groom, but make sure your speech doesn't delve into something that might upset or embarrass them too much. Also, don't talk specifically about any of the bride's or groom's exes. If you're not sure if you're crossing a line, ask another friend who knows the person well to read your speech ahead of time. I asked a fellow bridesmaid and one other friend to read my speech. I also got feedback from my sister, who knows my friend but was able to give me the "outsider wedding guest" perspective.

Keep it short - but not too short

Aim for at least a two minute speech, but don't talk for more than about ten minutes unless you're literally Tiffany Haddish or something (Hey lady, loved *Girls Trip!*). Three to five minutes is ideal.

Chapter Twenty-Three

ENJOYING YOUR DAY

Assuming you don't live in the path of an errant nuclear missile, your wedding day will eventually arrive! Marrying the sexy, feminist life partner of your dreams will probably be awesome on its own, but here are some other things you can do to make your day extra special.

Pick out a wedding scent

Studies have shown that scents are closely linked to memory, even more so than images. I do dresses, not science, so I'll leave that to *Psychology Today*: "Incoming smells are first processed by the olfactory bulb, which starts inside the nose and runs along the bottom of the brain. The olfactory bulb has direct connections to two brain areas that are strongly implicated in emotion and memory: the amygdala and hippocampus. Interestingly, visual, auditory (sound), and tactile (touch) information do not pass through these brain areas."[60] Sexy!

Because of this, you may want to wear a special new perfume or seek out other specific scents on your wedding day. Then, anytime you smell the scent in the future, you'll be taken back to your wedding day. You can shop with your partner for new fragrances, gift them to each other or even customize your own signature perfume or cologne at Le Labo, The Scentarium, Scenterprises, Waft or Unique Fragrance.

If perfume isn't your thing, you could diffuse some essential oil or light some candles in your bridal suite and then use the same scent at home

---

[60] Gaines Lewis, Jordan (Ph.D). "Smells Ring Bells: How Smell Triggers Memories and Emotions." *Psychology Today*. 12 Jan 2015.
https://www.psychologytoday.com/us/blog/brain-babble/201501/smells-ring-bells-how-smell-triggers-memories-and-emotions

anytime you want to trigger your memory. The scent of the flowers in your bouquet or even your wedding cake (sniff thoroughly!) could also do the trick.

Write a letter to your partner

It's easy to get caught up in logistics and entertaining your friends and family. Slow down a little by setting aside time on your wedding day to read a handwritten letter from your love (plan for both of you to write letters ahead of time). If there's something you want to say that you don't feel comfortable declaring publicly in your vows, a card or letter is the perfect place. Or maybe you can just write a bit more about why you're so excited to marry each other. Keep the letter to yourself or read it aloud after you're dressed to share it with your bridal party, photographer and videographer – these moments can be great additions to your wedding video, if you do one.

Find some time to be alone

Your wedding day will be a whirlwind. Try to schedule a specific time to be alone with your partner, like a quiet breakfast. Take a breath and soak it all in! If you don't want to see your partner until later, you might enjoy a sweetheart table at dinner for just the two of you instead of a big one with your entire bridal party.

If you're an introvert, you might also want to carve out some alone time in the morning before your friends, relatives and stylists descend on you like the Fab Five.

Eat

Many brides and grooms say they either forgot to or didn't have time to eat at their wedding. I find this viscerally offensive and urge you to shove more than just cake into your mouth.

David says, "My wife didn't eat enough food and felt really sick in the limo ride to our hotel after." Sexy!

If you've got a wedding planner or coordinator, ask him or her to save some food for you in case you end up walking around during dinner.

Adds Sean: "I wish we had known you don't actually have time to eat/drink at your own wedding. Would have snacked up a little beforehand."

Eat some actual food and pace yourself! "Don't eat two giant cupcakes. You might throw up on your wedding night," says Emily, who sounds like she knows this from experience.

Finally, stay hydrated. You can make a lifetime commitment but you can't remember to drink some damn water? SMH.

Pack a bag ahead of time

Don't wait until the last second to pack everything you need for your wedding, especially if you'll be staying away from your place the night before. One bride recommends that you put everything in a big box (remember Caboodles?!) and make the Best Man carry it around for you. Also, don't be afraid to ask your relatives or bridal party members to get emergency items from Target or CVS the night before or morning of your wedding.

Here's the ultimate list of what you might need to bring to your getting-ready space:

- rehearsal dinner outfit
- rehearsal dinner jewelry
- wedding gown
- veil
- bra
- underwear
- pasties
- shapewear
- lingerie/sleepwear
- outfit for the morning after
- shoes
- jewelry
- contacts/solution/case
- glasses/case
- eye drops
- toothbrush
- toothpaste
- breath mints/mouthwash
- facial cleanser
- face lotion
- body lotion
- deodorant
- perfume
- shave gel
- razor
- makeup
- compact mirror
- oil-absorbing blotters
- makeup remover/wipes
- sunscreen
- bug spray
- clear lip gloss
- detergent wipes/stick
- pen

- bandages
- shoe inserts
- sewing kit
- safety pins/buttons
- tooth wipes for wine stains
- pain-reliever
- prescription medication
- tampons/pads
- tissues
- bobby pins
- shampoo
- conditioner
- hair spray/mousse/gel
- hair dryer
- curling iron/straightener
- hand sanitizer
- nail polish for touch-up
- nail file
- nail clipper
- snacks
- water bottle
- pashmina/shawl
- parasol
- sunglasses
- keys
- wallet
- cell phone
- cell phone charger
- vows
- checks to pay vendors
- marriage license (if you don't drop it off ahead of time)

If you'll be getting ready away from your venue, you'll also want to have a clutch or smaller bag for essentials you want on-hand for the ceremony, reception and rides in between. You could also stock the reception space's bathroom with certain toiletries.

If you're going straight to your honeymoon, you'll need to pack for that as well. You might want to just bring everything with you to your wedding suite and then have a friend or relative take home what you don't need. If you don't HAVE to leave for your honeymoon immediately, you might want to take a day or two at home to regroup and reorganize.

Don't save too much for the final week

Most brides and coordinators recommend NOT leaving a lot of tasks for the week before your wedding. You'll be busy with final fittings, beauty appointments and arrivals of out-of-town family members and guests, so try to finish things like DIY décor and favor shopping at least one to two weeks ahead of your wedding day.

Put lots of information on your wedding website so that you won't be bombarded with last-minute texts about shuttles or dress codes. Don't be afraid to be specific about the dress code; tell guests you want men to wear ties and jackets if that's what you want. Restrictions like "no shorts" are also fine. "Don't dress to depress" might not mean the same thing to everyone. Some guests will forget about your website and annoy you with questions regardless, but don't be afraid to lean on your bridal party members for help with wedding week tasks – even texting crazy Dana from work.

Be yourself

On your wedding day, you should be the best version of yourself – not some unrecognizable person. "I wish someone had said to me, 'Wear your hair the way that you generally wear your hair.' That is, if you wear your hair down, have it down for your wedding," says Anastasiya. "This is a super specific regret I have about my own wedding, but it's something that makes a lot of sense in hindsight."

Similarly, if you never wear makeup, opt for a soft, natural makeup look instead of super dark lipstick and heavy eyeshadow. Be as glam as you like – and keep in mind that makeup that seems too heavy may look great in photos – but don't let anyone talk you into something that isn't you.

The *New York Times* reports that it's becoming more common for brides to go makeup-free (or nearly makeup-free) at their weddings.[61] Plain faces have always been acceptable for men, after all. If you want to get married without makeup, go for it! But one of the article's examples is a woman who flew an aesthetician to her wedding and got two facials with "masks and serums rich in collagen, placenta, antioxidants and anti-aging properties." I love a good facial, but isn't this just another kind of makeup? And if the idea is to make yourself live up to society's conventional beauty standards without any makeup at all, isn't that even more pressure? It's like Kate Beckinsale said – instead of wearing the corset, we're expected to BE the corset. Now we have to be the makeup, too?

Let yourself off the hook

---

[61] Strauss, Alix. "No Makeup on My Wedding Day." *The New York Times*. 18 April 2018. https://www.nytimes.com/2018/04/18/fashion/weddings/no-makeup-on-my-wedding-day.html

It won't be possible to witness every moment or have a long conversation with every guest at your wedding. Try to greet all your guests either by creating a receiving line or by going from table to table during dinner. But if these greetings are short, that's okay! Your guests understand that you have a lot to do. See if you can squeeze in some good convos at the rehearsal dinner (or welcome dinner, if applicable) so that you won't feel obligated to say a lot more during the reception. Also, remember that your photographer will capture everything, so you don't have to run around trying to be everywhere at once.

Remember that things will go wrong

It's just a fact. Ideally, snafus won't be on the level of "we got diarrhea from the shrimp," but you should be prepared for the fact that people make mistakes and forget things sometimes. Be flexible and don't let these "fun" surprises ruin your night!

"My caterer didn't pay as much attention to detail as I liked, but it was all little things like forgetting to refill the snacks on the tables during dinner," says Jen, who didn't let this spoil her wedding. And if worse things happen, you're not alone:

"For wedding #2, I woke up with a horrible stomach bug and thought I would have to go to the hospital, but luckily the family that ran the place had some home remedies," says Carolyn. "I had enough time to rest since the wedding day was pretty low key."

"A couple of hours before the photographer was due to arrive, one of the groomsmen called to say he had forgotten his suit jacket at his Airbnb in Queens [when the wedding was on Long Island]," Francesca says. "I said, 'No problem. Groomsmen will just wear their vests instead of suit jackets, no biggie.' The suit jacket took a ride in an Uber from Queens to the venue in time for photos. No one was the wiser."

Another bride told me that two of her relatives pretended not to see the table numbers on their place cards so that they could sit with the "artists and actors" at her wedding. They had to be escorted to the proper table!

Finally, Gina says she once saw a drunk dude projectile vomit across the room. "We had to bring in a hose," she says. At least it was only the rehearsal dinner? I hereby give you permission to freak out if this happens to you.

Don't hate on the weather

"It rained on an outdoor wedding," Kait says. "I was distraught and then complacent and then happy."

There's so much else for you to focus on, like the fact that you actually found a life partner you don't hate! Don't worry if the climate doesn't cooperate. Your photographer will be able to snap amazing photos no matter the weather.

Keep red rose petals off the floor

I asked a venue manager what mistakes she's seen couples make and she said, "Don't spread real red rose petals across a light-colored deck or floor – they will stain!"

Don't try new grooming treatments

"I tried to get a straight razor shave for the first time and my face burned like hell for the whole day after," says David. You can't enjoy your day if your skin or body parts are reacting to something new and strange. Only do treatments you've done before (you can always do a test run a few months early).

Check sports schedules

"Depending on your family/guests, see when football or other sports are played on your potential day," says Emily. "A friend got married on a huge college rivalry football weekend and most guests were on their phones instead of enjoying the reception." I have seen this first hand, too: I was once in a wedding where the Best Man was watching a college football game on his phone during the ceremony rehearsal. Maybe this wouldn't bother you – but if it would make you want to tackle people, choose a date without any sporting events.

Double-check everything.

"Things almost went wrong when our planner approved the proof of our wedding invite that had the wrong date on it," says Carolyn. "Luckily, the printer caught it.

"I screwed up our favors, which were engraved wedding glasses," says Beth. "There was a typo and we had to order them again. Totally my fault. Lesson, ladies: don't make important choices when you are exhausted and distracted!"

Chapter Twenty-Four

LICENSES, NAME CHANGES AND OFFICIANTS

Marriage Licenses

As much as we'd like to think marriage is about love and tulle, it's a regulated act that requires a license, just like fishing and boating. Romantic!

Marriage license policies vary by location, so your first step is to decide the city, state and country in which your nuptials will take place. You generally can't use a marriage license from one U.S. state to get married in another; similarly, marriage licenses issued in a Canadian province can only be used in that province. However, you can typically use a marriage license from one county to get married in a different county in the same state.

Next, do a quick internet search to find out where you'll need to apply for a marriage license in person, such as city hall or the town clerk's office. In Seattle, you must go to the Recorder's Office, which I assume involves a lot of hip baristas who play charming, flute-like instruments.

Some localities allow you to apply for a marriage license online or print out paperwork to fill out at home, but you will likely need to at least pick up the license in person. Most offices require that both you and your partner are present (some Canadian provinces only require one person, though.) You will also both need to know your Social Security number and bring picture identification. You might also have to bring divorce papers or a death certificate (if widowed).

Time your visit accordingly; in Washington State, marriage licenses are valid for six months, but in Massachusetts and Florida, they're only good for

60 days. States also enforce a waiting period – typically three days, but sometimes as long as 20 – before you can get married, so you can't rush to get a license the day before your wedding, unless you live in South Carolina, which only has a 24-hour waiting period. Las Vegas, NV has no waiting period at all – perfect for procrastinators and impulsive pop stars!

If you apply for your marriage license by mail or online, you might have a deadline by which you must pick up the license – it's commonly 10-15 days after your license is issued. Finally, don't forget to bring your marriage license to your wedding (or give it to your officiant ahead of time)!

Local government websites also generally provide other helpful information about marriage requirements. For example, you can't marry your first cousin in Washington – try New Mexico instead! Some states also require that one or two witnesses be present for your wedding ceremony.

Currently, Montana is the only U.S. state that requires a blood test - for female applicants without a waiver.

You will need to pay a fee of around $60-100 for your marriage license (but Florida will drop that down to $32.50 if you take a premarital course).

If you're getting married in a foreign country, obtaining a marriage license there can be complicated. To make things easier, you may want to get *symbolically* married at your ceremony and then get legally married at your local courthouse when you return home. If you want to get legally married in Italy or Mexico, for example, you'll need to have your original birth certificates translated into Italian or Spanish by a certified translator. (The same goes for divorce papers and death certificates.) In Mexico, you'll also need a blood test. And you'll still have to legalize your marriage when you return to your home country. Check your destination's tourism board website for more information.

Licensing Your Officiant

Your wedding officiant, who is in charge of swiftly filing your marriage license after your wedding, needs a license as well. This is also called becoming ordained. If you're hiring an experienced officiant, he or she will already have a license. But if you want a friend or family member to marry you, s/he can become ordained through a variety of nondenominational or interfaith online ministries, such as Universal Life Church or Open Ministry. A fee may be required. Before anyone pays to become ordained, though, confirm that the organization is registered and legit. Also, make sure your officiant allots enough time to become ordained, since it may take a few weeks to receive the official paperwork.

Changing Your Name

Should you change your name? It's a decision many women struggle with. Are you submitting to a patriarchal tradition or just being pragmatic? Is hyphenating to Rabinowitz-Tomasello going to make Kindergarten a nightmare for your kids?

According to *The New York Times*, the practice of keeping your maiden name rose in the 1970s, declined in the 1980s, and then rose again in the 1990s and 2000s. Now, about 20% of women who have recently married have kept their names, and around 10% of women chose a third option, such as hyphenating their name or legally changing their name while continuing to use their maiden name professionally.[62]

Today, the choice is less of a political or feminist act and more of practical one. Many women no longer feel that they need to keep their maiden name to prove a point, but they also don't see a name change as an invalidation of their independence or professional success. Changing all your social media accounts is super annoying, as is informing all your co-workers and clients of a name change. And if you've already established a career with your current name, you might worry about whether people can find your work history online.

"I chose to legally change my name, partly so I would have the same name as my future kids, and partly because I thought my husband's last name was cute," says a bride from Los Angeles, CA. "But professionally, I kept my maiden name, because I felt like it was memorable and helped people connect me to my work."

"Growing up, I always thought I'd change my last name," says Jen. It was just what you did. When I had to decide, I asked my fiancé his thoughts. He responded that no one was asking him if he was going to change his last name. He wanted me to do what I wanted to do. It made me love him even more. Then, I decided to keep my last name because it's who I am. It doesn't hurt that I like my last name, too!"

Some couples feel that sharing a name makes them a unit and makes it easier to do things like make hotel reservations. On some level, the name change is less about you and more about how strangers see you. People can make assumptions about your relationship when you share a name. But ultimately, if you keep your name, the world won't end. You and your partner have already figured out how to function as a couple with different names. Couples may also want share a name for when they have children, though

---

[62] Cain Miller, Claire and Willis, Derek. "Maiden Names, on the Rise Again." *The New York Times*. 27 June 2015.
https://www.nytimes.com/2015/06/28/upshot/maiden-names-on-the-rise-again.html

brides who already have children may want to keep their names for that reason as well.

Many brides told me that changing their name was more difficult than they expected. First, be careful when planning your honeymoon, since the name on your flight reservation must match the name on your picture I.D. Unless you are significantly delaying your honeymoon, you will probably want to make reservations under your maiden name, since your passport and credit cards will still have this name on them.

To make everything easier, decide if you're going to change your name *before* you apply for a marriage license. Most marriage license applications will allow you to change your name as part of the same process (but laws vary by location).

If you decide to change your name after you've already gotten a marriage license, you will need to file a name change petition at the same place you obtained your marriage license. You will also need to provide a certified copy of your marriage certificate. A fee may be required.

Next, you'll need to file your name change with the Social Security office and the Department of Motor Vehicles. If you have a passport, you'll also need to file forms with the State Department's Bureau of Consular Affairs. Finally, don't forget to change your name with your bank and creditors.

If you decide to turn your maiden name into your middle name, the process could be a lot more complicated. One bride found that she had visit several offices in person to make this switch.

Sound like a nightmare? You can hire a company like Hitch Switch to do it all for you – for a price, of course.

Epilogue

HOW TO TELL YOUR BOYFRIEND YOU'RE WRITING A WEDDING BOOK

Remember the philosophy professor from OKCupid?

Ten months into her Year of the Weddings, this hopelessly single wedding book writer met a guy.

It all started when I was at a housewarming party, eating an alarming amount of brie and lamenting the state of dating apps with one of my other single friends. Bumble has made men lazier! People don't even put words in their profiles! How does L.A. have so many clearly unemployed "CEO/Founders"?

"I just read an interview with a dating expert," my friend told me. "She said OKCupid has the most accurate algorithm. If you find someone on there who's over a 90% match and you actually think they're attractive, you should absolutely meet them in person."

Could it be true?

Well, it's been several months and the professor and I are still debating ethical conundrums over McConnell's ice cream. He's smart and thoughtful and sweet – and I assume I will soon discover that he's an alien who's come to Earth for reconnaissance or a more sinister mission. Pray for me, readers. Light me a candle. Soy, LED, I don't care. Maybe just tweet me a candle emoji. I'll take whatever you got.

I figured I'd better keep my wedding project a secret. How do you tell the guy you've only just started dating that you're writing a book about weddings? He's probably afraid of something serious! He's going to think you're obsessed! He's going to run for the hills (AKA unceremoniously ghost you)!

"There's something I haven't told you," I began, hoping his mind would jump to incurable STDs, and my news would come as a relief. "I'm writing a book about weddings." I then claimed that I was "DEFINITELY NOT OBSESSED WITH WEDDINGS," which I'm sure was very convincing.

I waited. I hoped.

"I can't believe you haven't told me this," he said.

Oh shit. It's over.

But then he smiled. And he didn't unceremoniously ghost me! He was merely surprised that I didn't tell him about such a big writing project. Because he supports what I do. What. A. Concept.

I realized that writing a book about weddings is nothing to be ashamed of. Instead of carefully strategizing to keep a man, isn't the feminist thing to find a man who respects you and your decisions?

Wanting a perfect wedding is nothing to be ashamed of, either. You can be a feminist and still think weddings are bomb. Stay strong, sister. Stop trying to please everyone. DIY your weird little heart out. Make your lizard the ring bearer. It's okay to say no. It's okay to say yes.

You do you!

Appendix

WEBSITES & RESOURCES

For clickable links to all these websites, you can get the e-book version of this book at amazon.com/author/amandapendolino .

General (Planning, Vendors, Venues, Budgets)

A Practical Wedding
Brides.com
Bridal Guide
The Budget Savvy Bride
Carats and Cake
Cost of Wedding
Here Comes the Guide
The Knot
Offbeat Bride
Reddit – Wedding Planning
Wedding-Spot
Wedding Wire
Woman Getting Married

Visual Inspiration

100 Layer Cake
Green Wedding Shoes
Junebug Weddings
Martha Stewart Weddings
Pinterest
Ruffled
Style Me Pretty
Wedding Chicks

Décor (including DIY)

Amazon
BHLDN
Etsy
JOANN Fabrics
Michaels

Party City
Target
Wal Mart
Wayfair

Creating Your Wedding Website

Appy Couple
Bliss & Bone
Cordially
eWedding
Joy
The Knot
Minted
Riley & Grey
Say I Do
Wedding Jojo
Wedding Window
Wedding Wire
Wedding Woo
Wix

Invitations, Stationery & RSVP Collection

anRSVP
Basic Invite
Evite
Minted
Paper Culture
Paperless Post
Paper Source
Papyrus
Postable
RSVPify
Shutterfly
Vistaprint
Zazzle

Preowned Gowns & Décor

Bravo Bride
Bridal Garage Sales
Craigslist

eBay
Facebook Marketplace
Poshmark
Preowned Wedding Dresses
Ruffled Recycled Your Wedding
Still White
Tradesy
Wedding-Recycle

Bridal Gown Designers

Adrianna Papell
Alessando Rinaudo
Alexandra Grecco
Allure
Amsale
Amy Kuschel
Anais Annette
Anna Campbell
Anne Barge
Aria
Berta
BHLDN
Calla Blanche
Carol Hannah
Casablanca
Catherine Deane
Christos
Claire La Faye
Claire Pettibone
Coco Melody
Da Vinci
Daughters of Simone
David's Bridal
Dear Heart
Divine Atelier
Eddy K
Elizabeth Dye
Ella Rosa
Emmy Mae
Enzoani
Essence of Australia
Galia Lahav

Heidi Elnora
Houghton
Ines di Santo
Isabelle Armstrong
Ivy & Aster
Jaclyn Jordan
Jane Hill
Jasmine
Jenny Packham
Jenny Yoo
JLM Couture
Justin Alexander
Karen Willis Holmes
Kate McDonald
Kelly Faetanini
Kenneth Pool
Kenneth Winston
Lace and Liberty
Laudae
Le Chateau
Leanne Marshall
Lela Rose
Limor Rosen
Louvienne
Lovers Society
Made with Love
Madison James
Maggie Sottero
Marchesa
Matthew Christopher
Mia Solano
Mon Cheri Bridals
Monique Lhullier
Moonlight
Mori Lee
Nicole Miller
Nurit Hen
Paloma Blanca
Peter Langner
Pnina Tornai
Pronovias
Rebecca Schoneveld
Reem Acra

Rish
Rivini
Romona Keveza
Robert Bullock
Rosa Clara
Rue de Seine
Sally Eagle
Sarah Seven
Sareh Nouri
Sincerity
St. Patrick
Stella York
Sweetheart
Tadashi Shoji
Tara Latour
Tara Lauren
Tatyana Mereynuk
Theia
Truvelle
Watters
Val Stefani
Venus
Your Dream Dress (online discount store)

Plus-Size Bridal Gown Designers

Allure Women
Anne Barge Curve Couture
Bohemian Curves by Rish
Callista
David's Bridal
Essence of Australia
Femme by Kenneth Winston
Maggie Sottero
Mori Lee Julietta
Roz La Kelin
St. Patrick White One Plus
Theia Curve
Watters & Wtoo

Bridal Boutiques That Specialize in Plus-Size Brides (or Have Specific Departments)

All My Heart Bridal (Lee's Summit, MO)
The Belle Bridal Boutique (Reading, OH)
Bombshell Bridal Boutique (St. Clair Shores, MI)
Bridal Bells (Berlin, CT)
Brides by Young (Indianapolis, IN; Schaumburg, IL)
Cherry Blossom Bridal (Washington, DC)
Curvaceous Couture (Columbia, MD)
Curvique (Austell, GA)
The Curvy Bride (Manalapan Township, NJ)
The Curvy Bride Boutique (Tulsa, OK)
Curvy Rose (Fayetteville, GA)
David's Bridal (national)
Della Curva (Tarzana, CA)
The Dress (Medina, OH)
Haute & Co Bridal Boutique (Chicago, IL)
Ivory Bridal (Atlanta, GA)
Kleinfeld (New York, NY)
Koda Bridal (Mt. Lebanon, PA)
Luxe (Egan, MN)
Mae Mae (New Orleans, LA)
Marry & Tux Bridal (Nashua, NH)
NY Bride & Groom (Charlotte, NC)
Olivia's Bridal House (Houston, TX)
Panache (Pasadena, CA)
Strut (Long Beach, CA; Tempe, AZ)
Unveiled Bride (Escondido, CA)

Other Dress Stores

Adrianna Papell
Asos
Barneys New York
Barneys Warehouse
Bloomingdales
Bluefly
Lulus
Macy's
Modcloth
Neiman Marcus
Neiman Marcus Last Call
Nordstrom
Nordstrom Rack
The Outnet

Revolve
Saks Fifth Avenue
Saks Off Fifth
ShopBop

Bridal Accessories

A.B. Ellie
Bel Aire
BHLDN
Bling!
Blossom
Brides and Hairpins
David's Bridal
Edward Berger
Elizabeth Bower
Ellen Hunter
Emma Katzka
Erica Koesler
Etsy
Everything Angelic
Haute Bride
Hushed Commotion
Jennifer Behr
Laura Jayne
Lia Terni
Lindsay Marie Design
Lori London
Malis-Henderson
Margaret Rowe
Marionat
Melinda Rose
Naturae Design
Ossai
Sara Gabriel
Ti Adoro
Twigs and Honey
Untamed Petals
The Wedding Outlet

Bridesmaid Dresses

Adrianna Papell
Alfred Sung
Allure Bridesmaids
Asos
Azazie
Bari Jay
BHLDN
Bill Levkoff
Bohoo
Colour by Kenneth Winston
Da Vinci
David's Bridal
Dessy
Hayley Paige Occasions
Impression Bridal
Jenny Yoo
Joanna August
Kennedy Blue
K-Mart
Lane Bryant
Lulus
Macy's
Modcloth
Nordstrom
Quiz
Sorella Vita
Two Birds
Watters
Weddington Way
Venus
Yelp (local stores)

Tuxedos & Suits

Banana Republic
Bloomingdales
Club Monaco
J. Crew
Kohl's
Lord and Taylor
Macy's
Men's Wearhouse
Nordstrom

The Black Tux
Yelp (local stores)

Dress Rentals

Hera Rentals
Rent The Runway
Union Station
Vow to Be Chic

Bride Gifts, Bridal Party Gifts & Wedding Favors

Beau-Coup
BHDLN
David's Bridal
Dynamite
Eros Wholesale
Etsy
Inkhead
Kate Spade
The Man Registry
Not on the High Street
Oriental Trading
Shutterfly
Things Remembered
Vistaprint
Wedding Favors Unlimited
Wholesale Favors

Wedding Registries

Amazon
Anthropologie
Bed, Bath & Beyond
Bloomingdales
Crate & Barrel
Honeyfund
Macy's
My Registry
Pottery Barn
Target
The Knot's Newlywed Fund
Wal Mart

Wayfair
Williams Sonoma
Zola

Online Ministries For Officiants

Open Ministry
Rose Ministries
Universal Life Church
Universal Ministries

Other

Hitch Switch
The Jewish Wedding Now by Anita Diamant

Marriage Licenses

Marriage license links for each U.S. state
https://family.findlaw.com/marriage/marriage-license-requirements.html

Marriage license links for each Canadian province
https://smartexpat.com/canada/how-to-guides/family/weddings-civil-partnerships/marriage-requirements

Marriage license info for the UK
https://www.gov.uk/marriages-civil-partnerships

Marriage license info for Australia
https://www.australia.gov.au/information-and-services/family-and-community/relationships/getting-married

ABOUT THE AUTHOR

AMANDA PENDOLINO lives in Los Angeles. She enjoys yoga, ice cream and *Say Yes to the Dress* (obvi).

Find out more (and please review this book!) at
amazon.com/author/amandapendolino

To receive information and updates, join Amanda's mailing list:
amandapendolino.com/wedding-planning-for-the-busy-feminist

Follow Amanda on Twitter: @amandapendo